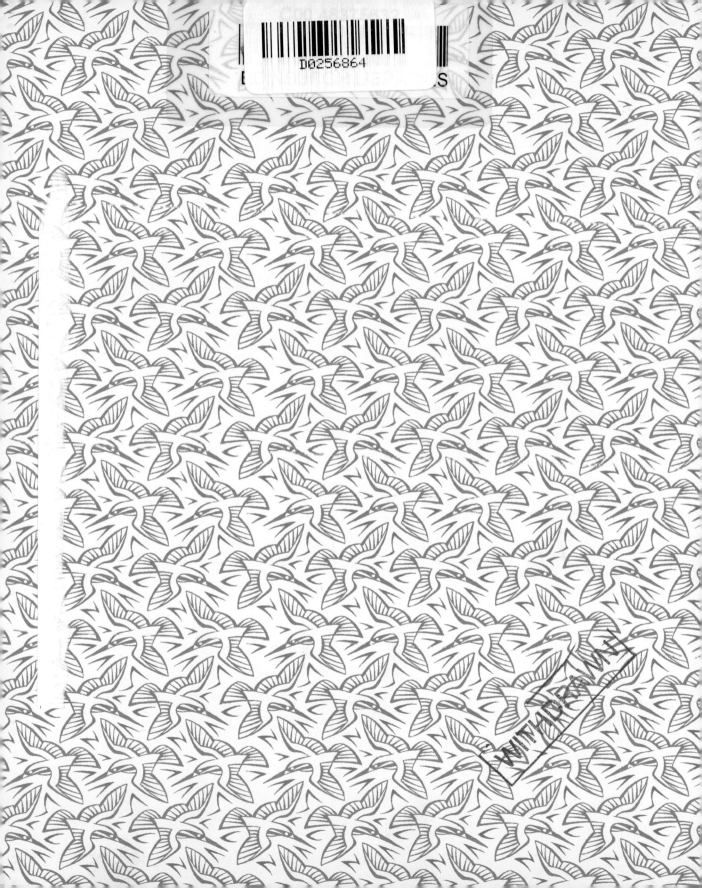

AS KINGFISHERS CATCH FIRE

AS
KINGFISHERS
CATCH
FIRE

Books & Birds

ALEX PRESTON
&
NEIL GOWER

corsair

CORSAIR

First published in Great Britain in 2017 by Corsair

1 3 5 7 9 10 8 6 4 2

Text copyright © 2017 by Alex Preston
Illustrations © 2017 by Neil Gower

The moral right of the author has been asserted.

Book design by Nico Taylor – LBBG

Grateful acknowledgement is made to the following for permission
to print previously published material:

'The Nightingale in Badelunda' by Tomas Tranströmer, taken from *New Collected
Poems*, trans. Robin Fulton (Bloodaxe Books, 2011)

'The Cage' by Osip Mandelstam, taken from *The Moscow and Voronezh Notebook*,
trans. Elizabeth and Richard McKane (Bloodaxe Books, 2003)

'Swallows' by Kathleen Jamie, taken from *The Tree House* (Pan Macmillan, 2004)

'Wild Geese' from *Dream Work*, copyright © 1986 by Mary Oliver. (Used by
permission of Grove/Atlantic, Inc. Any third party use of this material, outside of
this publication, is prohibited.)

'Listening to Collared Doves' by EJ Scovell, taken from *Collected Poems*.
(Reprinted by kind permission of Carcanet Press Limited, Manchester, UK.)

'Starlings, Broad Street, Trenton, 2003' by Paul Muldoon, taken from
Horse Latitudes (Faber and Faber, 2006)

'The Christmas Robin' by Robert Graves, taken from *The Complete Poems*. (Reprinted
by kind permission of Carcanet Press Limited, Manchester, UK.)

A CIP catalogue record for this book
is available from the British Library.

ISBN: 978-1-4721-5224-4

Printed and bound in China

Corsair
An imprint of
Little, Brown Book Group
Carmelite House
50 Victoria Embankment
London EC4Y 0DZ

An Hachette UK Company
www.hachette.co.uk

www.littlebrown.co.uk

AP: To Ary, Al and Ray.

NG: To my parents, John & Lindsey.

CONTENTS

INTRODUCTION

M Y FIRST MEMORY OF a bird and I'm lying on a picnic blanket aged four or five, watching a robin bounce across the grass towards me. I looked into that black and questing eye and felt a kind of fascinated horror at the otherness, the un-humanness of the bird. Those 'frightened beads' that Emily Dickinson wrote about 'that hurried all abroad' were both a challenge and a caution, telling me the robin would always perceive me as a potential predator, would never accept me as a friend. He was as different, and as enchanting, as the dinosaurs whose pictures covered my walls back then; perhaps I sensed the link between the robin and his reptile ancestors. 'Feather-light, hollow boned, full of song . . . Birds were like dinosaurs' better selves,' Jonathan Franzen said. 'They had short lives and long summers. We all should be so lucky as to leave behind such heirs.'[1]

Birds resist anthropomorphism, whatever Richard Bach's *Jonathan Livingston Seagull* would have you believe.[2] They are rarely caught or held, they flee when we want them close. 'They know suffering and joy in simple states not possible for us,' wrote J.A. Baker, one of the guiding spirits of this book. 'Their lives quicken and warm to a pulse our hearts can never reach. They race to oblivion. They are old before we have finished growing.'[3] This was what drove my birdwatching – the wish to collect something that was always just out of my grasp, to capture and catalogue my fleeting and sublime encounters with birds, in the air and on the page.

Birds are envoys from the world's hidden places. In *The Secret Garden*, it's a robin that shows Mary the way into the clandestine paradise that lies behind the high walls of Misselthwaite Manor. She had 'stepped close to the robin, and suddenly the gust of wind swung aside some loose ivy trails, and more suddenly still she jumped toward it and caught it in her hand. This she did because she had seen something under it – a round knob which had been covered by the leaves hanging over it. It was the knob of a door.' It's also a bird – a hermit thrush – that leads the narrator of T.S. Eliot's 'Burnt Norton' into the overgrown rose garden. Birds sing from the lost, loved corners of our childhoods, the green worlds that we have left behind.

As a boy, I followed the song-paths of birds, dragging my parents off to salt-swept estuaries and whispering reed beds, rising before dawn to couch myself in dusty hides or on the banks of slow-flowing rivers. 'Just be good and listen to birds,' advises the crow in Max Porter's *Grief is the Thing With Feathers*, and this is what I did. Like Wordsworth in 'Lines Written in Early Spring', I didn't understand the birds, but they delighted me.

> The birds around me hopped and played
> Their thoughts I cannot measure:
> But the least motion that they made
> It seemed a thrill of pleasure.

I surrounded myself with bird books, with Collins, Audubon and Peter Scott's *World Atlas of Birds*. My greatest joy, though, was the leap from the page to the sky, when the birds I'd seen illustrated on paper were there in front of me, rising into the wild sovereignty of the air. I remember an eagle, viewed from a boat on Loch Ness, and the feeling that my heart was lifting with it. I was like Josie in Dave Eggers' *Heroes of the Frontier*, for whom the eagle provides a model of escape. 'It was up, rising like it was nothing, flight was nothing, the planet was nothing, nothing at all, just another place to leave.' Watching birds was the best kind of play – serious, expansive and self-dissolving.

Then adolescence arrived with a thud, and suddenly girls, Nirvana and skateboarding began to elbow birds towards the exit door, a creeping sense of shame suffusing everything bird-related.[4] I slept late. I put my Barbour and binoculars in the understairs cupboard. I eschewed the quiet camaraderie of the bird hide, the Young Ornithologists' Club, the nature reserve with its taciturn, bearded wardens. You can never really stop seeing birds once you've been a birdwatcher, though. The peripheral impositions of birds on your consciousness (unnoticed by some, perhaps most) will always set some ancient-feeling instinct aquiver. You will wake early in strange houses and hear the reckless joy of the dawn chorus building in the air, and you will note how it differs from other choruses – the dominance of the blackbird or the song thrush, the under-notes of robin or wren – and you won't mind the ungodly hour. If, like Keats, a sparrow should come before your window, you'll drop down into its sparrowy world, 'take part in its existence and pick about the gravel.'

Because, although I stopped making 5 a.m. trips to Pagham Harbour to stand looking at curlews in the rain, I never stopped seeing birds and hearing them. I began to hunt for them when pursuing the great love that replaced birdwatching for me: books. At first almost unconsciously, but then with the same earnest application I gave to the birds of my childhood, I filled notebooks with poems and snippets of ornithological fiction or nature writing. Where once I had loved seeing the birds of my bird books in the open air, I now drew happiness from encountering birds I'd known in the wild ensconced on the page. That thrill of recognition from catching sight of a bird on a branch, I now found in poetry, in the nature writing of Annie Dillard or William Fiennes, in that perfect final stanza of Edward Thomas's Adlestrop:

> And for that minute a blackbird sang
> Close by, and round him, mistier,
> Farther and farther, all the birds
> Of Oxfordshire and Gloucestershire.

In the best bird writing – precise, light-filled, transporting – I came close to that childhood dream of possessing the birds, of having a world made up of feathered things.

Thumbing through my oldest notebooks now, I come upon, in a fifteen-year-old's scrawl, a passage from Daphne du Maurier's *Frenchman's Creek*:

> The beeches would be warm where the sun shone all day, and the river itself full and limpid with the tide. There would be sanderling skimming the rocks, and oyster-catchers brooding on one leg by the little pools, while higher up the river, near the creek, the heron would stand motionless, like a sleeping thing, only to rise at their approach and glide away over the trees with his great soundless wings.

The heroine, Dona St Columb, is enchanted by the special stillness of the birdwatching pirate, the Frenchman. She admits that ' ... before I came to Navron I thought very little about birds ... I suppose that – that the desire to know about these things was always present, but lying dormant.' It is the Frenchman who undertakes her ornithological education and soon, to the churring of nightjars, they are in love.

One other early note (and this, perhaps, because I admired the bird so much as a child, in all its Muscovite finery) recorded a death – in the opening lines of John Shade's poem in Nabokov's *Pale Fire*:

> I was the shadow of the waxwing slain
> By the false azure in the windowpane.[5]

Du Maurier and Nabokov are, perhaps, not obvious places to start (that would be – what? – Shelley's skylark or Chaucer's 'Parliament of Fowles' or Ted Hughes's *Crow*), but they illustrate the necessary element of partiality in this book, both in the poems and prose I've selected and in the birds represented.[6] I want writing that sets off little detonations of recognition, that makes the birds take shape in the mind in a way that is new and yet immediately familiar. As John Clare practised 'dropping down' to ground level to see the world from new perspectives, I want poets who are forever 'rising up' to view life from the bird's eye. I'm looking for what Gerard Manley Hopkins called 'instress' – when a writer manages to capture the 'inscape' of a bird, the disparate elements that make each creature identifiably unique, expressing what Hopkins described as its 'simple and beautiful oneness'. Paul Farley does this brilliantly in 'The Heron':

> One of the most begrudging avian take offs
> is the heron's *fucking hell, all right, all right,*
> *I'll go to the garage for your flaming fags*
> cranky departure

Gillian Clarke delivers the curlew's inscape in a line: 'She dips her bill in the rim of the sea . . . '[7]; Hopkins himself captured it when writing of kingfishers catching fire. This is why you'll find a lot of Ted Hughes and Mary Oliver here, a lot of John Clare and Kathleen Jamie. Gilbert White, W.H. Hudson and Richard Jeffries lead the prose writers, with Richard Mabey, Helen MacDonald and J.A. Baker their modern heirs. Many other descriptions of birds I've omitted either because they don't feel true to me or because I don't know them; if the portraits of birds in this book succeed it's because they come from a common source: a life in love with birds, where my encounters in literary ornithology have been every bit as important as the real thing.

The Chinese poet Bai Juyi, writing in the Tang Dynasty around the time King Alfred was being born in Britain, spoke of birdsong in a poem called 'Hearing the Early Oriole'. The poem's narrator is in exile, lying in bed, when a bird begins to sing on the roof of his house, causing him to think of 'the Royal Park at dawn'. Bai's narrator finds it hard to believe that the oriole he hears can be the same bird that had caused him to pause for a moment in his work at the palace:

> The bird's note cannot really have changed;
> All the difference lies in the listener's heart.
> If he could but forget that he lives at the World's end,
> The bird would sing as it sang in the Palace of old.[8]

One of the sparks for this book was a bird memoir given to me by my father. It was written in the late 1920s by Edward Grey, my grandmother Ursula's great-uncle (if you can follow that). The book was called *The Charm of Birds* and was about how watching and listening to birds had helped to soften the series of losses and setbacks that Grey suffered in his eventful life. He was the longest-serving British Foreign Secretary, heavily involved in the build-up to the Great War, a complex man who found happiness in the sight and song of birds. *The Charm of Birds* spoke to me across the decades, providing a model for the kind of book that this one might be: literary (Grey was obsessed with Wordsworth, whom he called 'Big Daddy'); conversational (reading Grey's book you feel as if you're sitting in an armchair with the great statesman after a port or two); genially meandering (the organising principle for *The Charm of Birds* is ostensibly the months of the year, but actually it's whatever Grey's voracious curiosity settles upon next). More than anything, Grey writes of the power of birds and their song to act upon the human spirit, transforming interior and exterior landscapes, fixing memory to place.

I have started birdwatching again now I've reached my thirties. I think many come back to birds at this age; partly it's that we're comfortable in our skins by now, no longer dealing in the tawdry economy of teenage kudos. It's also that we need new ways to define ourselves as we move towards middle age, pursuits to fill the hours of our free time; we reach for the things that delighted us when we were young. Birdwatching is a good frame to hang a life upon and that's what I've done. What's more, after almost two decades spent as a literary birdwatcher, I find my encounters with birds in nature imbued with rich new resonances, as if all the poets of the canon were crammed into the hide with me, describing what I see.

If this book works as I want it to, it'll appeal to birder and non-birder alike. I'd love it to be as vital a companion to ornithologists as their field guides, illuminating all the webs of meaning, of joy that birds spin out behind them: triangulating between the bird, the world and literature. It should say something about the beauty of precision in writing, the importance of style, the merits of close looking, and these things should speak to you even if you don't know a crow from a corncrake. I realise that it's ended up as neither anthology nor memoir; neither literary criticism nor nature writing; but a bit of all of these. It's not quite the book I meant to write, but, as Iris Murdoch said, 'every book is the wreck of a perfect idea.'

Edward Grey didn't get around to penning his autobiography, but then he didn't need to: *The Charm of Birds* was a record of his life, smuggled into a bird book. I feel that, almost accidentally, I've ended up writing something that tells more truths about me than perhaps I wanted it to, and for the tangents and footnotes, the memories and inward life, I hope you'll forgive me. I've been harbouring this book for decades and seeing it come together, with Neil's exquisite illustrations like perfect crystallisations of the chapters I've written, has been overwhelming. This book is, above all, a history of the deep joy that comes from looking up and writing down.

PEREGRINE

I BECAME A BIRDWATCHER IN October 1986. It was half-term, I was seven, and we'd rented a farmhouse on the Isle of Wight, just outside Freshwater. My aunt Jo came – she now lives on a remote stretch of the Florida coast where, from an Art Deco veranda, she watches ospreys dive and manatees rise. She'd brought her binoculars on the holiday and we went out together, along the cliffs and across the estuaries, and I learnt a way of looking at the world – landscape filtered through the birds that flew above it – that coloured it forever.

Our last morning on the island, I walked out alone, up past Tennyson's house at Farringford, to the wild whaleback of land that arches down to the Needles.[1] It was early and the dew was ablaze in the sunlight that poured over the grass towards the chalk pinnacles in the distance. There was a cliff below me, its foot a roil of raging sea. And then, as if the sky had been rent in two, a bird stooped, diagonally, devouring the air, and my world was never the same again. My aunt would later tell me that it was a peregrine, but all I remember was that it came down like the head of a shovel flung from the heavens.[2] Pure velocity. I hadn't read Tennyson back then, but if I had, I would have thought of his eagle who:

> watches from his mountain walls
> And like a thunderbolt he falls.

The bird dropped and dropped, a blue comet trailing tawny fire, until it disappeared into the salt spray below.

In her first book of prose, *Falcon*, Helen MacDonald uses Franz Boas's concept of *Kulturbrille* – culture-glasses – to describe the complex manner in which we perceive the natural world. Our birds are never just birds but are constructed from any number of disparate sources – literature, art, folklore. She picks this up again in *H is for Hawk*, with reference to J.A. Baker's *The Peregrine*, published in 1967. MacDonald says that 'most of my bird-loving friends read Baker's book before they saw a live one, and now they can't see real peregrines without them conjuring distance, extinction and death. Wild things are made from human histories.' Robert Macfarlane confirms this theory, noting in *Landmarks* that 'When I have seen peregrines I have seen them, or I remember them, at least partly in Baker's language.'

There's no more intimate link between bird and book than the peregrine in Baker's prose-work. I hadn't read it when I saw my first, that brilliant blue bird spearing the October sky, but such is the immersive experience of *The Peregrine* that it's not only coloured everything since, but has re-shaped my memories of the three or four peregrines I saw before reading it. I can't think, or write, about these birds without borrowing Baker's distinctive linguistic tics.[3] Language forms worlds – Proust's Combrey, Hemingway's bullfights, Edmund de Waal's netsuke, Baker's peregrines.

Baker was an enigmatic figure, a tenebrous presence in his own book, a vector through which his four Essex peregrines spoke.[4] In *Falcon*, Macdonald presents the novel as an 'ecological *Confessions of St Augustine* or modern-day Grail-search, these are at heart the diaries of a soul's journey to grace . . . ' By the time she comes to write *H is for Hawk*, her stance towards the book has hardened. There are many similarities between T.H. White's *The Goshawk* and Baker's *The Peregrine*, but while the former sparks the recovery that Macdonald records, she 'saw no hope at all' in *The Peregrine*. It was:

> the writer's awful desire for death and annihilation, a desire disguised
> as an elegy for birds that flew through poisonous skies, falcons as

searing-bright and pewter-flashed as reflected sun, already things of memory before they were ever gone.

The Peregrine is not a comforting book. Where Baker does appear, his presence is overwrought, his tone elegiac. 'I have always longed to be part of the outward life,' he writes at one point. He wanted:

> to be out there at the edge of things, to let the human taint wash away in emptiness and silence as the fox sloughs his smell into the cold unworldliness of water; to return to town a stranger. Wandering flushes a glory that fades with arrival.

The Essex saltings that Baker's four peregrines stalk are dreary and *unheimlich*; the narrator's melancholy spirit, like that of W.G. Sebald (another doleful East Anglian wanderer) infects the landscape it describes: 'The sun fired the bone-white coral of the frosted hedges with a cold and sullen glow.'

The Peregrine reveals something important about birdwatching, though. In his introduction to my NYRB Classics edition, Macfarlane says that it's 'not a book about watching a bird, it is a book about becoming a bird.' Baker's *I* even merges into *we* at one point, the human as one with the falcon. When he reaches these heights of deep communion, Baker is able to escape the prison of himself. The falcons become companions in misery, friends with whom to be alone – parallel players. And we get the sense that, in losing himself in the falcons, Baker finds a weight lifted from his twisted body:

> I shut my eyes and tried to crystallise my will into the light-drenched prism of the hawk's mind ... I sank into the skin and blood and bones of the hawk ... Like the hawk, I heard and hated the sound of man, that faceless horror of the stony places. I stifled in the same filthy sack of fear. I shared the same hunter's longing for the wild home none can know, alone with the sight and smell of the quarry, under the indifferent sky. I felt the pull of the north, the mystery and fascination of the migrating gulls. I shared the same strange yearning to be gone.

If you read *The Peregrine* as the literal record of one winter's falcon-watching, you'd end up a dispirited birder. Not only has Baker condensed a decade's experience into a single October-to-March, but the intimacy and proximity with which he renders his 'hawks' gives the impression they're performing for him in a private diorama of marsh and sea and sky. The book has endured, though, because it tells another kind of truth, about the sublimity of watching birds, the gateway they provide to another world. The risky language that Baker mints to lend voice to his peregrines (and to his experiences watching them) is testament to the power of the birds, to the contortions of the brain required to find words sufficient to describe them in all their wildness.[5]

Macfarlane is spot on when says that this is 'a book in which little happens, hundreds of times.' What makes *The Peregrine* compelling, rather than stulti-fying, is how Baker's language shapes each new encounter with the bird, like a musician performing variations on a theme, or a painter addressing the same subject again and again, straining towards perfection.[6] The peregrine is 'like the winged helmet of a Viking warrior,' it's 'a shark's head dropping from the sky,' it flies in 'that cloud-biting anchor shape, that crossbow flinging through the air.' The bird's plumage at first 'gleamed like a shield of silver water, glowed purple-brown and wet like dark ploughland after rain;' then 'above, they were the colour of the sea's deepest blue; below, like the soiled whiteness of shadowed chalk.' I copied out countless passages from *The Peregrine* into my notebooks, finding some new excitement of language or observation on almost every page, but I'd choose this as my favourite, if only for that final, exquisite, image of the 'falling nets of starlings':

> He circled higher, then stooped languidly down, revolving as he fell, his golden feet flashing through sunlight. He tumbled headlong, corkscrewing like a lapwing, scattering starlings. Five minutes later he lifted into air again, circling, gliding, diving up to brightness, like a fish cleaving up through warm blue water, far from the falling nets of starlings.

In 2013, I went back to the Isle of Wight for the first time in almost thirty years. It was Evie Wyld's wedding. Her family owns a stretch of wooded land between Yarmouth and Freshwater, on top of which sits a ruined folly — a temple of canted columns and cracked arches. It was the most beautiful July, the island drenched in golden light, and we led Evie and Jamie down the aisle with instruments and singing, and then sat and drank and danced and watched the sky fade above England.

The next day, I took my wife up to the Needles. We looked over Totland and Alum Bay, and just saying the names was a way of bringing the past before us. If I were J.A. Baker, I'd tell you of the peregrine we saw, dropping down over the headland, taking a pigeon in flight and then extending its wings to the sun like a blue crucifix. I might have quoted Peter Reading to my wife. In his 'Laertidean', Reading writes of seeing a peregrine stooping:

> into a blizzard of wheeling *Calidris Alba*[7]
> and the falcon hit and we heard the thud and a handful of silven feathers
> whorled in the wind and the great dark raptor rose with the dead meat
>   locked in its talons;
> and I said to my friend: 'We will mind this as long as we live.' (He is dead
>   now.)

I might have quoted Chaucer's *The Squire's Tale*, in which Canace, the daughter of Genghis Khan, uses a magic ring to speak with a peregrine she finds bleeding in a leafless tree and who tells the princess about her faithless tercelet, who has abandoned her for a kite.

A faucon peregryn thanne semed she	A falcon peregrine she was, and she
Of fremde land, and everemoore	Seemed from a foreign land;
as she stood	and as she stood
She swowneth now and now for	She fainted now and then for loss of
lakke of blood,	blood,
Til wel neigh is she fallen fro the	Till she had almost fallen from
tree.	the tree.

But we didn't see a peregrine, nor anything much save the rich long grass pulsing in the breeze, the sunlight exploding on the water and on the cliffs, boats like tethered balloons on the horizon. It was enough, though, to be there and to remember my first peregrine, because that's another thing birds do for us – they give narrative to a landscape, they fix the world to a fleeting truth.

SWALLOW

S WALLOWS NEST IN MY aunt Gay's bedroom. From mid-March onwards she, a spinster, beautiful and eccentric, leaves the windows of the stone farmhouse in which she lives open to the wind and rain and, never later than the fifteenth of April, the arrival of:

> A blue-dark knot of glittering voltage,
> A whiplash swimmer, a fish of the air.[1]

The house sits under the brow of a long hill in the Charentais countryside, peering through trees to a river. There are ten dogs, a dozen horses who occasionally clop through the kitchen to eat your breakfast over your shoulder, but the place only feels inhabited once the swallows come. Whenever I'm there, I find myself thinking of Roger Deakin, who wonders 'if the swallows that nest in the chimney of my Suffolk farmhouse have the faintest idea how profoundly they affect my emotions. When they first arrive from the south in spring, and I hear the thrumming of their wingbeats amplified to a boom by the hollow brickwork, my heart leaps. They seem to bless the house with the spirit of the south; the promise of summer.'[2]

They're first seen darting around the eaves of my aunt's house, filling the early morning with what the Greek poet Anacreon called their 'tuneless serenade'. They fly quiveringly in 'that touchingly inefficient way, where their whole body is like this violent opening and closing of a book'.[3] Then they begin to weave their coracle-like nests along the lintels of my aunt's bedroom. Ted Hughes sees these nests as a 'hand stretched from under the eaves',[4] and Kathleen Jamie 'a home-/made bracket of spittle/ and earth'.[5] Soon they are flitting through the farmhouse like thoughts, flashing streamers of iodine blue. 'She flicks past, ahead of her name,' says Hughes in 'A Swallow'; in 'Swallows II', he claims that:

> What is loveliest about swallows
> Is the moment they come,
> The moment they dip in, and are suddenly there.

This is how it is at my aunt's house: the swallows arrive and the atmosphere lifts, as if buoyed by their beating wings, the chatter and reproach of their song. They spatter their chalky white shit on the floorboards, on the heavy provincial furniture, on a stand of gaudy hats. In the evenings, they scissor through the room one last time as the light fades, then hand the night on to the bats. 'Their last sweeping flight of the day,' writes Tim Dee, 'turned imperceptibly from hunting sorties, hawking after insects, to a final minute of more sweeping flight of great beauty, back and forth.'[6]

We didn't always believe in the miracle of migration. Gilbert White, who greeted the swallows in excited Latin: '*Hirundo domestica*!!!', thought swallows hibernated in ponds for the winter.[7]

> It is worth remarking that these birds are seen first about lakes and mill-ponds; and it is also very particular, that if these early visitors happen to find frost and snow, as was the case in the two dreadful springs of 1770 and 1771, they immediately withdraw for a time. A circumstance this, much more in favour of hiding than migration; since it is much more

probable that a bird should retire to its hybernaculum just at hand, than return for a week or two to warmer latitudes.

John Clare, in 'On Seeing Two Swallows Late in October', half-hopes they might last out the winter, if not for their sakes, then for his:

> I wish ye well to find a dwelling here,
> For in the unsocial weather ye would fling
> Gleanings of comfort through the winter wide,
> Twittering as wont above the old fireside,
> And cheat the surly winter into spring.

It is possible to figure the swallow's migration as a kind of wandering, in penitence or hope, a heartbroken *Fernweh*. In Joyce's *Portrait of the Artist as a Young Man*, Stephen Dedalus associates himself with the swallow – 'birds always coming and going' – while Byron in 'The Siege of Corinth' calls the swallow 'A wild bird and a wanderer'. In Oscar Wilde's 'The Happy Prince', the Swallow (a male in Wilde's tale, a female – *la golondrina* – in Borges's Spanish translation of the story) dies rather than leave its friend, the Prince, who sends gifts to the poor and wretched of the town via his winged messenger. As winter sets in, the Swallow dies:

> 'It is not to Egypt that I am going,' said the Swallow. 'I am going to the House of Death. Death is the brother of Sleep, is he not?' And he kissed the Happy Prince on the lips, and fell down dead at his feet.

In my own novel *In Love and War*, Esmond, an exiled Englishman trapped in wartime Florence, sees swallows arrive in April 1942. He stands above the swimming pool in the villa where he's holed up and watches as the birds:

> threw themselves down over it to drink from the reflections of their beaks. Esmond imagined them flying up in a great dark wing over

the desert where brave sunburnt soldiers stared across a landscape of dunes and mirages of the enemy. When summer ended, they'd swoop – on sudden instinct – southwards to the desert and the dying. The sand would be crossed with bones, dark blood, husks of tanks and troop-carriers. If the swallows knew anything at all, he thought, they'd weep as they passed over, or fly north, back into frozen whiteness.

I remember swimming in my aunt Gay's pool, golden summer evenings, when swallows would arrow down to dip their beaks in the water, their tawny breasts dyed turquoise, then rise up to inscribe giddy arabesques upon the air. It was these swallows, exactly, that I was seeing in my mind as I wrote the passage above. That dizzy dance away from the earth also captivated the poet Leonora Speyer. She was a migrant herself, who'd fled London for New York after anti-German attacks on her husband, and loved swallows because they, too, escaped.

> They hover and lean toward the meadow
> With little edged cries;
> And then,
> As if frightened at the earth's nearness,
> They seek the high austerity of evening sky
> And swirl into its depth.[8]

It's true that there's a skittish flutter in their flight, but as you walk across the fields that surround Gay's farmhouse, beneath 'sharp swallows in their swerve / flaring and hesitating / hunting for the final curve,'[9] the birds also seem to be envoys of a kind of freedom. In Peter Hobbs's beautiful novel *In the Orchard, the Swallows*, which turns upon the image of a girl under a swallow-filled sky, the narrator, imprisoned, watches the birds from his cell window. 'They are so quick, so perfect in their lines, like little miracles in the air.' In a similar vein, the German writer and dissident Ernst Toller, elegised by Auden after his suicide, wrote in *Das*

Schwalbenbuch of the swallows who would build their nests in a prison in Bavaria. When the nests were destroyed by prison guards, the swallows built again, their steadfast application in the face of dumb brutality giving hope to the inmates:

> Let Europe chant the praises of her aeroplanes,
> But I, Number 44,
> With all the silent music of my heart,
> Will praise the flight of swallows.[10]

There's a certain day each June when my aunt wakes to silvery morning light and the rising sound of new life from the nests. In 'Augury', Caitriona O'Reilly writes of the moment the eggs hatch, revealing their 'staring cargo: six bronze bibs, / six black-masked, African birds.' It is deemed good luck to have swallows nesting in your house, although swallows build their nests in the sails of Cleopatra's ships in Shakespeare's *Antony and Cleopatra* and 'the augurers say they know not, they cannot tell; look grimly, And dare not speak their knowledge.'

Towards the end of Homer's *Odyssey*, Minerva turns herself into a swallow, perching on a rafter as she directs Odysseus's battle against the suitors of Penelope. We have long granted swallows these gifts, vatic powers, and in return their paths scribble messages in the sky. In *The Rings of Saturn*, W.G. Sebald writes of:

> ... the summer evenings during my childhood, when I had watched from the valley as swallows circled in the last light, still in great numbers in those days, I would imagine that the world was held together by the courses they flew through the air.

Tim Dee sees swallows 'describing in the air the shape of a rope or a rein by which all things might have been tied under the sky.'[11] Hughes defines their flight as a 'Foreign sort of sky-writing ... / Everything a signature and a flourish',[12] while Howard Nemerov, in his poem 'The Blue Swallows', figures their tails as nibs, dipped in ink, writing 'Some cabalistic history / Whose authorship you might ascribe / To God?'

I imagine Aunt Gay, a wilful woman who lived most of her peripatetic youth on horseback, waking in the first light of dawn and watching her swallows flicker across the room. I think of the way that the swallows have become the children she never had, those fragile lives building around her in mud-and-clay cups. I imagine her pinning her dreams to them. I think of Yeats and Lady Gregory:

> They came like swallows and like swallows went,
> And yet a woman's powerful character
> Could keep a swallow to its first intent.

I think of Gay's mother, my late grandmother Ursula, and of William Maxwell, who borrowed Yeats's lines to write about his own dead mother in *They Came Like Swallows*. I imagine that Gay's swallows call back to her the swallows of her childhood in England and how they beckoned her south – to Africa, to Italy and then to France.

When I first read Kathleen Jamie's 'Swallows', I felt an absurd jolt of recognition: it was my aunt's house, the narrator my beloved Gay. The sonnet seemed to spin past my conscious mind, so that I slid down through the words into the morning brightness of Gay's room, the dark radiance of her smile and that effervescent stream of summer birds. I copied Jamie's poem into a notebook and I'll recite it like a blessing the next time I step into the swallow-strewn air of that room.

> I wish my whole battened
> heart were a property
> like this, with swallows
> in every room – so at ease
> they twitter and preen

from the picture frames
like an audience in the gods
before an opera
and in the mornings
wheel above my bed
in a mockery of pity
before winging it
up the stairwell
to stream out into light

KINGFISHER

A MEMORY THAT SPEAKS IN the language of dreams: a kingfisher, so bright above the river it seemed aflame. We were camping in the New Forest, our battered VW Combi under the arms of an oak. The campsite was called Sandy Balls, which made me and my brother giggle. I left my family playing chess and set off into dense, silent woodland, stepping over rills of water, mossy boughs, through waist-high bracken. I was eight years old. Finally, coming out onto some minor tributary of the Avon, I lay down on the warm, tussocky bank, lifted my binoculars and waited.

Arrows of sound came shooting down the river seconds before the flash of light. A 'tail-less hologram', an 'azure lizard' as Chris McCabe puts it; or a vision 'escaped from the jeweller's opium', for Ted Hughes in 'Kingfisher'. The bird pulled up downstream where the river widened and the waters flowed slower. Perched on a twig, he peered into the brindled shallows, and I call him now to mind in John Clare's words:

> In coat of orange green and blue
> Now on a willow branch I view
> Grey waving to the sunny glean
> King fishers watch the ripple stream

For little fish that nimble bye
And in the gravel shallows lie.

I watched him as he dove, then dove again, this time coming up with a glistening minnow in his long black beak, his wings trailing droplets of silver-green water. Back on the twig he necked the fish and then he was gone, and I never saw him again.

This kingfisher, maybe four months after my Isle of Wight peregrine, was another of the founding incidents of my birdwatching life, a moment of sublimity that sustained me through so many other, less fruitful trips. When, in D.H. Lawrence's *The Rainbow*, Ursula Brangwen escapes her parents for the first time, she walks through the woods until she comes to a river:

> She saw a kingfisher darting blue – and then she was very happy. The kingfisher was the key to the magic world: he was witness of the order of enchantment.

The sudden brilliance of my own kingfisher held out something similar – it promised a lifetime of encounters with birds like this, in solitude, worlds of secret and awful beauty.

A kingfisher appears again in another Lawrence story, 'The Shades of Spring'. The hero, Syson, now married and living in town, returns home to visit his childhood sweetheart, Hilda. Their relationship had been built around a mutual love of birds and so, when they meet again, they take up their childish ways:

> She showed him nests of robins, and chaffinches, and linnets, and buntings; of a wagtail beside the water. 'And if we go down, nearer the lake, I will show you a kingfisher's . . .'

It soon becomes clear to Syson, though, that Hilda has changed; she is now 'very womanly', twenty-nine and betrothed to a gamekeeper. They argue and part, and Syson wanders dejectedly into the woods until he comes upon a stream:

> Threads of brown water trickled by, touched with gold from the flowers.
> Suddenly, there was a blue flash in the air, as a kingfisher passed.
> Syson was extraordinarily moved . . . What a wonderful world it was –
> marvellous, for ever new.

Three centuries earlier, in his country-house poem 'Upon Appleton House', Andrew Marvell wrote of coming through woods (like Syson, like Ursula, like me) to a river and there seeing a kingfisher.[1] Here his enraptured description of the bird presages another arrival – that of his tutee, the daughter of the house, Maria Fairfax. Of the 'modest Halcyon', he writes:

> The viscous Air, wheresoe're She fly,
> Follows and sucks her Azure dye;
> The gellying Stream compacts below,
> If it might fix her shadow so;
> . . .
> And Men the silent Scene assist,
> Charmed with the saphire-winged Mist.

Halcyon, the bird's alternate name, comes from the Greek ἀλκυών – Alcyone, a moon goddess associated with the solstices who, when Zeus killed her husband, Ceyx, tried to drown herself and was turned into a kingfisher. The Latin name of the bird, *Alcedo Atthis*, refers to a beautiful young woman beloved of Sappho. One of Sappho's fragments, 'To Atthis', begins: 'Atthis has not come back to me: truly I long to die.' Both names speak to the the solitary, melancholy beauty of the bird.

I've seen other kingfishers, probably more than my allocated share (no one is permitted more than a portion of that kind of loveliness), and remember one that flashed past by the side of a lake in Gloucestershire. I was walking, my two-year-old son in a backpack behind me, through gloomy winter woods, the leafless trees dripping with mist, no sound except the distant grumble of the A44. We came to open water and there, skimming the lake, flying, as Marvell puts it in 'Upon Appleton House', 'Betwixt the air and water', was the kingfisher. It seemed particularly incongruous, this vision shimmering against the grey and listless winter day, 'as if an azure bolt from a crossbow had been suddenly shot across our path,' as James Harting has it. In 'Kingfisher', the poet Peter Scupham describes a similar walk, everything damp and dreich until the bird arrives:

> And then, from wastes of stub and nothing came
> The Kingfisher, whose instancy laid bare
> His proof that ice and sapphire conjure flame.

It wasn't far from my hibernal sighting that T.S. Eliot set the first of his *Four Quartets*, 'Burnt Norton'.[2] Here, picking up from Milton and Hopkins, he imbues the kingfisher with symbolic significance, linking the bird to the figure of the Fisher King.[3] It is a poem about time and finds a way of stopping it in the mad flutter of the kingfisher's wings, the bird trapped for a brief moment under the nib of the pen:[4]

> After the kingfisher's wing
> Has answered light to light, and is silent, the light is still
> At the still point of the turning world.

It's a beautiful image in a poem which opens with the speaker being led into a rose garden by a thrush, then expelled from this paradise, and ends with the kingfisher offering a kind of consolation – the possibility of halcyon days snatched from the winter storm, light and silence freed from the noise of time.

The American poet Charles Olsen used the image of the kingfisher to take on Eliot and his ideas about tradition. 'The kingfishers! / who cares / for their feathers / now?' he asks at the beginning of his long poem *The Kingfishers*. In it, he demonstrates how much violence there is bound up in the idea of tradition, explaining that, behind the beauty of the kingfisher – 'he got the color of his breast / from the heat of the setting sun!' – is a base and ugly life of murder and bones.

> It nests at the end of a tunnel bored by itself in a bank. There,
> six or eight white and translucent eggs are laid, on fishbones
> not on bare clay, on bones thrown up in pellets by the birds.
>
> On these rejectamenta
> (as they accumulate they form a cup-shaped structure) the young are
>   born.
> And, as they are fed and grow, this nest of excrement and decayed fish
>   becomes
>   a dripping, fetid mass

Olsen's poem seems to tap into a fundamental mistrust of the bird, as if by appearing like 'the pixelated dash from Victorian taxidermists', [5] it must be hiding some dark shame or secret sorrow. It reminds me of the words of the forgotten Victorian naturalist Charles Coward, whose work is notable largely for the scorn he pours on the birds he writes about (and the tame army of boys who bring him specimens and eggs). 'On the whole,' he writes, 'the kingfisher is only tolerable on account of the beauty of its plumage.'

It may be that the kingfisher – so fleeting, so fickle – reminds us of our own distance from such grace. It may be that the bird, whose average lifespan is barely a year and who is so vulnerable to frosts and foul water, carries some tragic air about him. It may be that things of such beauty are always a little sad. Whichever, there are few who can write of the bird as blithely as Clare and Marvell.

With a note of desperation, Mary Oliver reprises Hopkins's kingfisher catching fire in her poem 'The Kingfisher', but finds no comfort, despite the bird's splendour, in being one of the dying generations. 'I think this is / the prettiest world,' she writes, 'so long as you don't mind / a little dying.' W.H.

Davies sees the solitary launches of the kingfisher as something to attach his own loneliness to, identifying with a bird prone to choose 'For haunts the lonely pools, and keep / In company with trees that weep.'

We end up with a quite different picture of the bird, far from Eliot and Hopkins's comforting Christian symbolism, far from the kingfishers that lift Lawrence's characters from their private sorrows, different also from the bright lance of light it drives in my memory. Here is a bird dwelling in a rancid bone-crypt,[6] living a life of lonely divagations along wintry rivers, alone with its terrible beauty. Only Ted Hughes, I think, can synthesise the two visions, ending with a portrait of the kingfisher that is brutal and beautiful, sacred and real.

> Through him, God, whizzing in the sun,
> Glimpses the angler.
> Through him, God
> Marries a pit
> Of fishy mire.

KESTREL

MY AMERICAN GRANDPARENTS STAYED in Hampstead when they came to London, sometimes for academic summers, sometimes for year-long stretches when my grandfather was on sabbatical from Princeton and working on a book. They rented a cottage winged onto the white villa of the music critic Hans Keller and his wife, the German artist Milein Cosman. Milein was a warm, benevolent presence in my childhood, a gifted painter who'd send us Christmas cards she designed herself. My daughter has one of her Venetian angels on her mantelpiece; the edition of Georg Trakl's poems Milein illustrated sits beside my bed. She's ninety-five now. My grandfather, aged ninety-two, still sees her whenever he's in the UK.

I have a photo of Milein taken at the Edinburgh Festival in 1947. Shot from above, in profile, you see her sketching Peter Ustinov, a deliberative smile on her face, a string of glass beads around her neck. This was the year she met Keller, less than a decade since she'd fled Nazi Germany and come to Oxford to study at the relocated Slade. It was in Oxford that she encountered Sidney Keyes, who (alongside Keith Douglas) was the greatest British poet of the Second World War. Keyes was captured by the Germans in Tunisia just before his twenty-first birthday and died in captivity, but he'd had time in his short life to write 110 poems, many of them addressed to Milein (who did not return his fervid, desperate love). In his poem 'The Kestrels' the birds in their wild freedom are Milein, while the poet is bound to the earth, at once resigned to the falcons' untamed nature and comforted by it — that Cosman will remain one of the world's fierce, unmastered things.

> When I would think of you, my mind holds only
> The small defiant kestrels—how they cut
> The raincloud with sharp wings, continually circling
> Above a storm-rocked elm, with passionate cries.
> It was an early month. The plow cut hard.
> The may was knobbed with chilly buds. My folly
> Was great enough to lull away my pride.
>
> There is no virtue now in blind reliance
> On place or person or the forms of love.
> The storm bears down the pivotal tree, the cloud
> Turns to the net of an inhuman fowler
> And drags us from the air. Our wings are clipped.
> Yet still our love and luck lies in our parting:
> Those cries and wings surprise our surest act.

The unruliness of kestrels has earned them a reputation as thuggish, *déclassé*.[1] They pick the bones of the executed in the Free City of Volantis in George R.R. Martin's *Game of Thrones*; 'kestrel' is used as a term of insult by Halbert Glendinning in Sir Walter Scott's *The Monastery*. Discovering Keyes's poem about Milein — finding, as it were, a wilder side to the smiling, grandmotherly figure who'd illuminated my childhood — helped also to rehouse the bird in my mind, to elevate it by association.

In her 1486 guide to gentlemanly etiquette, *The Boke of Seynt Albans* (otherwise known as *The Bokys of Haukyng and Huntyng; and Also of Coot-Armuris*), Dame Juliana Berens created a hierarchy of falconry, fitting a raptor on each rung of the social ladder:

An Eagle for an Emperor, a Gyrfalcon for a King:
a Peregrine for a Prince, & a Saker for a Knight,
a Merlin for a lady, a Goshawk for a Yeoman,
a Sparrowhawk for a Priest, & a Kestrel for a Knave.

T.H. White explains in *The Goshawk* that:

The *Boke of St. Albans* had laid down precisely the classes of people to
whom any proper-minded member of the *Falconidae* might belong ...
the list had defined itself meticulously downward to the kestrel, and he,
as a crowning insult, was allowed to belong to a mere knave – because he
was useless to be trained.

The kestrel, with his distinctive grey hood and stippled russet wings, is
Britain's commonest falcon, seen floating above suburban golf courses and
intercity railway sidings, harvesting the soft estates of multi-lane motor-
ways.[2] Orwell writes of seeing a kestrel 'flying over Deptford gasworks', while
Michael Longley pictures the bird happily surveying a man-made cityscape:

Because an electric pylon was the kestrel's perch
I wanted her to scan the motorway's long acre
And the tarmac and grassy patches at the airport.[3]

It's almost as if, having been deemed subaltern for centuries – T.H. White
named him 'the common churl, the medieval villein'[4] – the kestrel has made
himself at home in a modern world of commerce and industry, happier hovering above smoke-stacks and layby caffs than preening in jesses on a gauntlet.

The kestrel's working-class credentials are confirmed in Barry Hines's
A Kestrel for a Knave, filmed by Ken Loach as *Kes*. In the book, set over a
single day in the life of Billy Caspar in an unnamed Northern mining town,
our hero finds respite from tedium and toil in the sublime oscillations of his
kestrel. When Kes flies, he says, 'everything seems to go dead quiet'. The
kestrel also acts as a vehicle for Billy's rage at his brother Jud's bullying,

his father's absence, his mother's wantonness: 'Folks stop me and say, "Is it tame?" Is it heck tame, it's trained that's all. It's fierce, and it's wild, an' it's not bothered about anybody, not even about me right. And that's why it's great.' Billy's joy when he first sees a kestrel hover and dive for prey is glorious, infectious:

> 'I was right underneath it, then I saw its mate, it came from miles away and started to hover, just over there.' Billy started to hover, arms out, fluttering his hands. 'Then it dived down behind that wall and came up wi' summat in its claws. You ought to have seen it, mister, it wa' smashing.'

The Canadian poet Anne Wilkinson, like Billy Caspar, loved the kestrel for its wildness and wrote 'Falconry', a response to *The Boke of Seynt Albans'* snobbish dismissal of the bird:

> Rather bating[5] kestrel, I,
> Than mind the fist beneath the glove.
> I, a kestrel, God, the Knave—
> And I will bate until I die,
> And bite the leather of my jesses,
> And starve before I eat His messes.
> Can I do more? Sweet Knave, I'll try.

She admires the way the bird refuses to submit, the solitary 'bachelor peasant'[6] brutishness of him, the cruelty of the yellow bottle-opener beak.

It is as if, over the centuries, the kestrel and his knave have become one, and this union electrifies one of the strangest and most vivid passages in Edward Thomas's *The Icknield Way.* Thomas is walking through fields deep with snow when he comes upon a scene of slaughter, an omen. 'A kestrel had killed a gold-crest upon the bank, and as I approached it sailed away from the crimson-centred circle of feathers on the snow.' The knavish kestrel has killed the continent's smallest bird and now takes flight, soaring above the barn that is Thomas's destination. The bird's flight is linked to the motion of the wind upon the hills which has been:

> luxuriously, playfully carving the snow . . . The curved wind-work in the drift . . . remained in the stillness as a record of the pure joy of free, active life contented with itself. It was the same blithe hand which had shaped the infant born in this black barn.

Thomas is visiting Lone Barn, a tumbledown cowshed 'subject to the hostility of discontented spirits'. It is here that a vagrant with six children lived (a seventh born in the snow on Christmas Day), until the father was arrested for neglect and his family sent to the poor-house. Thomas rootles amongst the rags on the floor and finds the vagrant's journal. It turns out that the tramp, A.A. Bishopstone, was an Oxford man, his diary full of Flaubert and Blake, philosophy and religion. The final passage in the journal reads, 'I heard the wind rustle in the dead leaves this morning, I heard it rustle over my grave, and over the world's, and over the embers of all the stars, and I was not afraid.' The slaughter which introduces the scene taints the whole chapter, although it is unclear which of the birds represents Bishopstone – the journeyman kestrel or the innocent gold-crest.

The kestrel's hover, that exquisite moment when the bird hangs in the air, seeming to slow time as it dangles in the heavens and then drops, has captivated writers over the centuries.[7] Carol Ann Duffy describes the kestrel as treading air, while Virginia Woolf quoted Gilbert White in a *New Statesman* essay: 'The kestrel, or windhover, has a peculiar mode of hanging in the air in one place, his wings all the while being briskly agitated.' Richard Jeffries, in an 1884 essay on 'The Hovering of the Kestrel', attempts to maintain a studious, scientific distance in his field notes on the bird's flight, before breaking into a passage of extraordinary lyricism:

> He will and does hover in the still, soft atmosphere of early autumn, when the gossamer falls in showers, coming straight down as if it were

raining silk. If you puff up a ball of thistledown it will languish on your breath and sink again to the sward. The reapers are sweltering in the wheat, the keeper suffocates in the wood, the carter walks in the shadow cast by his load of corn, the country-side stares all parched and cracked and gasps for a rainy breeze. The kestrel hovers just the same.[8]

Gerard Manley Hopkins's 'The Windhover' is one of the greatest poems about any bird. It takes the kestrel's hover and builds it into a wild cascade of rhythm and imagery, until form and subject snap together like a falcon's beak. In *Seven Types of Ambiguity*, William Empson says the poem has the power to 'pierce to regions that underlie the whole structure of our thought; could tap the energies of the very depths of our minds.' Hopkins's poem is dedicated 'To Christ Our Lord', and it turns the bird hanging in the air into a complex figure: part benevolent God looking over his flock, part crucified Christ as hero, ready to swoop and save:

> dapple-dawn-drawn Falcon, in his riding
> Of the rolling level underneath him steady air, and striding
> High there, how he rung upon the rein of a wimpling wing.

Empson says the pivotal word in the poem is 'buckle', around which the meanings hinge and collect, the ambiguities so dense that the bird appears to be coming apart before its glorious plummet downwards:

> Brute beauty and valour and act, oh, air, pride, plume, here
> Buckle! AND the fire that breaks from thee then, a billion
> Times told lovelier, more dangerous, O my chevalier!

It's a time-stopping poem, a moment in which words and the kestrel's hover are one, and we can freely marvel – as Hopkins does – at 'the achieve of, the mastery of the thing'.

Like the earth-bound poet at the end of 'The Windhover' ('shéer plód makes plough down sillion[9] / Shine,'), the speaker of Ted Hughes's[10] 'The Hawk in the Rain' is caked in mud — 'I drown in the drumming plough-land'[11] — looking up at the pendulous hawk:

> Effortlessly at height hangs his still eye.
> His wings hold all creation in weightless quiet
> Steady as hallucination in the streaming air
> While banging wind kills those stubborn hedges

We sense again the quietness of the hovering hawk, of time stilled. There are echoes of Hopkins, but also of Yeats's falcon in 'The Second Coming': 'Turning and turning in the widening gyre / The falcon cannot hear the falconer.' The kestrel is about control, about man and wildness, about how, as Hughes puts it, 'the hawk hangs, / The diamond point of will.' Everything here strains and flexes, more masculine and visceral than 'The Windhover', paying tribute to darker, older gods. This is a poem whose heart is in 'the master- / Fulcrum of violence where the hawk hangs still.'

GULL

J OHN UPDIKE WROTE IN his journals of stretching out on a spit of
sand, looking up at a sky full of gulls. It was afternoon at Crane Beach,
just north of Boston, and he found himself struck by a 'spasm of inspiration'.
The gulls themselves seemed to dictate the first stanza of a poem to him:

> Penless and paperless, I ran to the site of a recent beach fire and wrote in
> charcoal on a large piece of unburned driftwood. Then I cumbersomely
> carried my improvised tablet home. It must have been late in the beach
> season, and my final stanzas slow to ripen, for the poem's completion is
> dated early December.[1]

The poem, 'Seagulls', begins:[2]

> A gull, up close,
> looks surprisingly stuffed.
> His fluffy chest seems filled
> with an inexpensive taxidermist's material
> rather lumpily inserted.

The first verses are an exercise in close looking – we're alongside Updike on the beach, lying back and inspecting 'the sardonic one-eyed profile, slightly cross'. The poem opens out into something larger and more ambitious as those later-composed stanzas unfurl, and we catch the note of nostalgia, the sense of a summer viewed from the tail of autumn, when the crowds have left and many of the gulls with them.

Updike writes of the hour towards the end of the day when 'flies begin biting in the renewed coolness', the sun casts the scene in a 'pink shimmer', and:

> the gulls stand around in the dimpled sand
> like those melancholy European crowds
> that gather in cobbled public squares in the wake
> of assassinations and invasions,
> heads cocked to hear the latest radio reports.

It's a wonderful image, glowing with the inner light of deep recognition, and leads us into a powerful final stanza, lending dignity to both the gulls and the pudgy lovers who walk amongst them.

> It is also this hour when plump young couples
> walk down to the water, bumping together,
> and stand thigh-deep in the rhythmic glass.
> Then they walk back toward the car,
> tugging as if at a secret between them
> but which neither quite knows –
> walk capricious paths through the scattering gulls,
> as in some mythologies
> beautiful gods stroll unconcerned
> among our mortal apprehensions.

Updike also manages to catch the shonkiness of the gulls, the sense that, like their land-lubbing *confrères* the pigeons, they are more likely to be warped or mangled, club-footed or broken-winged than other birds. He notes that:

> even the feather-markings,
> whose intricate symmetry is the usual glory of birds,
>   are in the gull slovenly,
> as if God makes them too many
> to make them very well.

Growing up by the sea, I remember dozens of injured gulls: broken wings, broken backs, birds pressed into the tarmac so many times they seemed part of the road. There's one whose image catches the breeze of memory and billows in my mind – a herring gull, hit by a car, flapping and scrabbling down the pebbles towards the sea, desperate and steely.[3]

Joseph Mitchell didn't write about wounded birds but about Joe Gould, a broken man who believed he could speak to them. Mitchell is a writer of narrative non-fiction whose visions of New York life have entirely refashioned and re-enchanted that city in my mind. He visited Gould twice in print, firstly in a short piece called 'Professor Seagull', then in a novella-length book, *Joe Gould's Secret*.[4]

Gould was 'a blithe and emaciated little man who has been a notable in the cafeterias, diners, barrooms, and dumps of Greenwich village for a quarter of a century. He sometimes brags rather wryly that he is the last of the bohemians.' Gould was born into a wealthy New England family, disowned when he came to New York to live his dissipated, writerly life. He was friends with e.e. cummings, praised by Ezra Pound, his work published in the *Dial* by Marianne Moore. His magnum opus, which he called his Oral History, supposedly ran to many millions of words, scribbled in notebooks hidden around the city. He lived on booze and ketchup and the handouts of a dwindling number of friends.

Gould called himself 'the greatest authority in the world on the language of the sea gull.' At the louche Greenwich Village parties in the 1920s and

1930s at which he was first welcome, then tolerated, then blacklisted from, he'd perform his seagull poetry, which Mitchell describes several times:

> He pulls off his shoes and socks and takes awkward, headlong skips about the room, flapping his arms and letting out a piercing caw with every skip. As a child he had several pet gulls, and he still spends many Sundays on the end of a fishing pier at Sheepshead Bay observing gulls; he claims he has such a thorough understanding of their cawing that he can translate poetry into it. 'I have translated a number of Henry Wadsworth Longfellow's poems into sea gull,' he says.

In *Joe Gould's Secret*, he gives a rendition of 'Hiawatha' in sea gull, in which he 'threw his head back and began to screech and chirp and croak and mew and squawk and gobble and cackle and caw, occasionally punctuating these noises with splutters.' Mitchell also charts Gould's efforts to join the Village's rather demure Raven Poetry Circle, recording the words of the president of the Circle, one Francis Lambert McCrudden, who said that Gould:

> isn't serious about poetry. We serve wine at our readings, and that is the only reason he attends . . . At our Nature Poetry Night he begged to recite a poem of his entitled 'The Sea Gull.' I gave him permission, and he jumped out of his chair and began to wave his arms and leap about and scream, 'Skree-eek! Scree-eek! Scree-eek!' It was upsetting. We are serious poets and don't approve of that sort of behaviour.

I think I love Gould as much as I love the herring gulls that ululated on the roof of my childhood home, or the gulls that wake me when I stay with my dad in Aldeburgh, shrieking their shanty operas on the roof of Benjamin Britten's house across the road. They're rakish and piratical, bullying and boisterous, commonplace but still glorious as they rise and cast themselves out over the sea.[5] In 'Thames Gulls', Edmund Blunden wrote of how, in gulls, we find the co-mingling of the everyday and otherworldly.

Friendly as stars to steersmen in mid seas,
And as remote as midnight's darling stars,
Pleasant as voices heard from days long done,
As nigh the hand as windflowers in the woods,
And inaccessible as Dido's phantom.

This is what Mitchell does with Gould – showing us the depth and dignity of the man as he rootles through trash cans or staggers from flop-house to flop-house. We sense the precariousness of life and the uncertainty of fame, and we feel we know Gould as one of us – his woundedness is like our own.

In her essay 'Bird', Mary Oliver writes of caring for an injured gull with her partner, the literary agent Molly Malone Cook,[6] at their home in Provincetown, Rhode Island. The gull was dying and wouldn't eat, but a deep bond built between the two women and the wounded creature. They called the gull Bird, and played games with him. Oliver would sit at the piano and play Schubert, Mahler, Brahms. Music made him quiet and, 'dipping his head, he would retire into the private chamber of himself.'

Oliver came to know Bird, to intuit deep truths about what it was to be a gull; she began to understand what made him happy, what would soothe him through the 'rough-and-tumble work' of his death. 'He was, of course, a piece of the sky,' Oliver writes. She knew because 'His eyes said so . . . Imagine lifting the lid from a jar and finding it filled not with darkness but with light. Bird was like that. Startling, elegant, alive.'

The end, when it comes, is as beautiful as it is inevitable. Oliver's final paragraph undoes me every time in its gathered-in dignity, its soft devastation. It is doubly moving now that M., as well as the gull, is gone and Oliver lives alone in their house overlooking the water.

But the day we knew must come did at last, and then the non-responsiveness of his eyes was terrible. It was late February when I came downstairs, as usual, before dawn. Then returned upstairs, to M. The sweep and play of the morning was just beginning, its tender colors reaching everywhere. 'The little gull has died,' I said to M., as I lifted the shades to the morning light.

It's a passage that brings to mind Oliver's most famous lines, from her poem 'The Summer Day':

> Doesn't everything die at last, and too soon?
> Tell me, what is it you plan to do
> with your one wild and precious life?

And it strikes me that looking after a bird until it dies, giving it some kind of dignity in death, there are worse answers to that question. Oliver says as much in 'For Example', a poem inspired by the injured gull.

> I love this world, even in its hard places.
> A bird too must love this world,
> even in its hard places.
> So, even if the effort may come to nothing,
> you have to do something.

Another wounded gull, another poet now better known for his prose: Edmund Gosse wrote one of the great memoirs of family life, *Father and Son.* In it, he recalled growing up with his stern, evangelical father, an early marine biologist who attempted to marry his own militant creationism to the evolving theories of Lyell and Darwin.[7] Gosse's father was severe and reserved: the day of Edmund's birth was recorded in his diary with typical distance: 'E. delivered of a son. Received green swallow from Jamaica.' Gosse's mother died when he was a child and his father immediately moved the family to Devon, where he'd be closer to the subjects of his scientific interest. Edmund grew up unhappy, lonely and under the shadow of his martinet father.

In one sense, 'The Wounded Gull' shows why Gosse has been remembered more for his memoir than his poetry: it is stridently Victorian, Kiplingish at its best, Alfred Austinean at its worst. It is perhaps only that it recalls to me my own dear, gentle father and how shaken he was whenever he had to put a creature out of its misery, and how this is one of the things we take on when we become fathers — one of the difficult, necessary tasks of adulthood.

We also get something more from the poem if we know Gosse's own history — the lonely, unloved boy on the rocky Devon shoreline, the sense of the sea calling to him. 'For a long time,' he wrote in *Father and Son,* 'no other form of natural scenery than the sea had any effect upon me at all . . . the moon of snow-white shingle and the expanse of blue-green sea.' The first stanzas show us the author revisiting the scene of his solitary childhood, this time with his own family in tow.

> ALONG a grim and granite shore
> With children and with wife I went,
> And in our face the stiff breeze bore
> Salt savours and a samphire scent.
>
> So wild the place and desolate,
> That on a rock before us stood —
> All upright, silent and sedate —
> Of slate-gray gulls a multitude.

They come across a wounded bird, separated from its fellows and flapping gamely towards the water.

> The children laughed, and called it tame!
> But ah! one dark and shrivell'd wing
> Hung by its side; the gull was lame,
> A suffering and deserted thing.

The bird sets out onto the rolling waves, where 'it could but die, and being dead / The open sea should be its tomb.' One can't help but feel Gosse there, alongside the gull as it paddles out into the roiling waters, its bravery something like his own as he struck out, badly damaged, from his father into the wild, Godless world. The poem attempts a kind of reflexive patriotism, but the final stanza brings it back to the personal, to Gosse and his family, to the bird facing death with a stiff British beak.

We watched it till we saw it float
Almost beyond our furthest view;
It flickered like a paper boat,
Then faded in the dazzling blue.

It could but touch an English heart,
To find an English bird so brave;
Our life-blood glowed to see it start
Thus boldly on the leaguered wave;

And we shall hold, till life departs,
For flagging days when hope grows dull,
Fresh as a spring within our hearts,
The courage of the wounded gull.

STARLING

ONE OF THE PUREST joys of my childhood was playing cricket in the road on seaside summer evenings and looking up to see a vast flock of starlings flooding the sky. They'd billow up from the sea-end of the street, emerging from the fringes of clouds that rose like mountains over the water, and flow in a great dark stream towards the South Downs. We'd all stop, crane our necks, falling silent as thousands of birds passed overhead, 'a writhing of imps / Issuing from a hole in the horizon.'[1] That magnificent murmuration lasted all of thirty seconds, and yet the game was never the same afterwards and we'd soon drift off to bed with the ataxic image of the birds shimmering in our young minds.

Coleridge spoke of 'a different Glory – Starlings –', and the sight of these ungainly, boisterous birds transformed in flight has become a staple of the poetic imagination, a short-cut to the sublime.[2] Perhaps it is that we recognise in their transmutation from doltish, solitary gutter-foragers into a vision of sky-borne unity the trailing edges of a forgotten dream. Maybe it's that we feel, like Mary Oliver in 'Starlings in Winter', that we might undergo some profound change, were we only able to cast off the shackles of earth.

> Chunky and noisy,
> but with stars in their black feathers,
> they spring from the telephone wire
> and instantly
> they are acrobats
> in the freezing wind.

I remember the shadow of a thick cloud of starlings that stippled the sheets of my son's cot as I drew curtains on an East London square some eight years ago. The evening's last light touched the tops of the bare trees and the birds were suddenly illuminated as they came in to roost. I found a poem by James McAuley, an Australian, and it reminded me of my baby boy, winter, and sun on starling feathers.

> As the sun lights up their coat
> Its metallic lustre glows,
> A blue burnish comes and goes,
> Iris glistens at the throat.[3]

We were happy in that higgle-piggle Hoxton house, with its rickety stairs and slanting floors. Occasionally starlings would come and perch on the window-sill as I worked and I'd look at them up close, seeing the rubies and emeralds that gleamed in their feathers, and then they'd be off, wheeling up into the trees, and I'd watch 'the starnels darken down the sky', as John Clare put it. At night we'd hear them chatter and shriek themselves to sleep, as:

> Ten thousand starlings are dreaming in the darkness
> about the sunlight over the fields.[4]

In her letters, Eudora Welty writes repeatedly of a favourite piece of prose, recommending that her friends buy Henry Green's *Concluding*, if only for the following description of starlings at dusk. It's an exquisite passage, luminous with perception, and I remember the feeling of having discovered something precious as I copied it into my journal one October evening.

> Then, as they came to where the trees ended, and blackbirds, before roosting, began to give the alarm in earnest, some first starlings flew out of the sky. Over against the old man and his granddaughter the vast mansion reflected a vast red; sky above paled while to the left it outshone the house, and more starlings crossed. After which these birds came in hundreds, then suddenly by legion, blank and blunt against faint rose. They swarmed above the lonely elm, they circled a hundred feet above, until the leader, followed by even greater numbers, in one broad spiral led the way down and so, as they descended through falling dusk in a soft roar, they made, as they had at dawn, a huge sea shell that stood proud to a moon which, flat sovereign red gold, was already poised full faced to a dying world.

This paragraph picks up on an earlier passage in the novel, where starlings rise from a wood, and we see with great vividness that swirling, eddying storm that starlings unleash upon the sky: 'they ascended in a spiral up into a blue sky; a thousand dots revolving on a wave, the shape of a vast black sea-shell pointed to the morning.' It's that seashell-shape that I look for now when I see starlings massing over the old, burnt-out pier on Brighton seafront, one of the few places I know where they still regularly throng. Green has given me new ways of seeing them, or has lent words and shape to something long-known but never spoken.

It was Juliana Berens who coined the phrase 'a murmuration of stares', an audible image which nonetheless captures the visual impact of the birds.[5] I remember that we were aware as kids, playing cricket under fading summer skies, of the noise that came a sliver of time before the pullulating swarm above, what Ted Hughes called 'a faint sky-roar / Of pressure on the ear', a soft starter pistol before the show. But it was the sight of them that left its mark upon us. Jesper Svenbro sees the murmuration as:

> myriads of swarming punctuation marks out there,
> starlings flying in formation,
> sudden sharp turns, steep ascents,
> swarm on delightful swarm
> against a rosy cloud bank in the east.

I studied 'A Glimpse of Starlings' by Brendan Kennelly at school. It was collected in one of those oddly capacious anthologies – *New Oxford English 3* – which I still have, its green cover bleached and slick with age. I copied out the poem into my first notebook and it moves me still, partly because it is such a decent, straightforward piece of writing, in which the narrator recalls his father, who died alone and ill – 'He doesn't know why his days finished like this'. But it's also that I studied it aged fourteen, at the very tail of my (first) birdwatching life, and it was one of the pieces that suggested to me a new direction for my interest in birds, the possibility of encountering them in literature now that I was no longer able to visit them in the wild. The teenage me read and re-read the brief lines about starlings at the end, which grant a final, hopeful note – of beauty in life, or the promise of an afterlife – to an otherwise desperately bleak poem:

> over his shoulder a glimpse of starlings
> Suddenly lifted over field, road and river
> Like a fist of black dust pitched in the wind.

Wolfgang Amadeus Mozart appeared relatively untroubled by his own father's death in 1787. The real mourning was reserved for three weeks later, when his beloved pet starling died. He'd purchased the bird from a Vienna market stall on 27 May 1784. It lived in his music room, soon learning to sing back to him his own compositions. Here he notes the beauty of its rendition of his Concerto in G Major – *Das war schön!*[6] – despite the fact that the bird sang an avant-garde G# half-way through.

Das war schön!

Mozart buried his starling, whose name has been lost to history, in a ceremony attended by dozens of heavily veiled mourners. The composer was undone by the bird's death and led the crowd in a procession, sang a series of specially composed hymns and then read this poem over the small, ebony coffin:

> Here lies a beloved little fool,
> A starling.
> Who, still in the prime of his life,
> Must taste death's bitter draft.
> Thinking of this
> My heart is rent in two.

In *Corvus*: *A Life With Birds*, Esther Woolfson describes adopting her own starling, a foul-mouthed bird called Max, whose 'complex, multi-layered, sweet evening song' brought back to her 'my Glasgow childhood of dark afternoons, twilight in a Scottish city, when phone wires were strung between poles, each like a necklace, richly decorated with bead-like rows of glittering starlings.' The same association of the bird with an urban soundscape illuminates Edwin Morgan's 'The Starlings in George Square'. It's a poem about the noisy birds who love 'the high stonefields' and 'the warm cliffs of man'. While the busy, commercial world is askance at the bustle and bruiting of the starlings – 'councillors place rubber plugs in their ears' – a man stops with his son and points up to a flock of the birds, which:

> scatters in swooping arcs,
> a stab of confused sweetness
> that pierces the boy like a story,
> a story more than a song.
> He will never forget that evening,
> the silhouette of the roofs,
> the starlings by the lamps.

My godfather, Ian, gave me a book when I was ten or eleven, at the peak of my bird-mania. Called *Shakespeare's Birds*, and written by the jolly-sounding Peter Goodfellow, it does very much what it says on the tin, listing, bird-by-bird, all of the species mentioned in Shakespeare. I used to refer to it before going to a play with my parents and listen out for the cormorant, or magpie, or snipe, giving a privileged little nod when the bird appeared. There's only one mention of starlings in the plays, when Harry Hotspur in *Henry IV Part One* comes up with a ruse to rile the king: train a starling to repeat the name of Mortimer, the Earl of March, a favourite of Richard II now kidnapped by Owen Glendower:

> I'll have a starling shall be taught to speak
> Nothing but 'Mortimer,' and give it him
> To keep his anger still in motion.

This single appearance had far-reaching consequences. The species was absent from the Americas until the 1890s, when Eugene Schiefellin's American Acclimatization Society released 120 starlings in Central Park, part of their efforts to establish the full avian cast of Shakespeare's plays in thc United States. Current estimates put the bird's population in the country at 200,000,000.

This bullying colonialism, where the starlings' territorial gains came at the expense of indigenous species, gave the birds a bad name in the States. Rachel Carson, author of *Silent Spring*, wrote that:

> In spite of his remarkable success as a pioneer, the starling probably has fewer friends than almost any othcr creature that wears feathers. That fact, however, seems to be of very little importance to this cheerful bird with glossy plumage and stumpy tail.

Starlings once flocked in similar numbers in the UK; in 1949 a flock alighted on the hands of Big Ben one June evening and, as if to remind the recovering city to look up at the hour when shadows fall, stopped the clock for five minutes.

In *The Emigrants*, W.G. Sebald's unnamed narrator describes the way the birds have coloured Manchester's late-afternoon landscape for him:

> Everything would then appear utterly unreal to me, on those sombre December days when dusk was already falling at three o'clock, whcn the starlings, which I had previously imagined to be migratory songbirds, descended upon the city in dark flocks that must have numbered hundreds of thousands, and, shrieking, incessantly, settled close together on the ledges and copings of warehouses for the night.

The bird's decline in Britain has been so precipitous that there are barely a million left in the country and it is now on the RSPB's red list.

The loss of starlings in the UK is felt like the death of a friend you expect to run into in old, familiar places. Uncanny, a downland sky without them. But these past weeks, as I've been reading and writing and thinking about starlings, I've begun to see them again. Not the swarming numbers of my youth, but a dozen or two wheeling over the park, a flock dancing on the eaves of a big, red Victorian school in Willesden. It made me realisc that the kind of attention you pay when you're reading helps you to see differently, to notice better and more precisely. I also picked up a copy of Paul Muldoon's *Horse Latitudes*, a collection I'd not read before, and in it found a sonnet, a breathless sentence: 'Starlings, Broad Street, Trenton, 2003'. The poem seemed to bring together all that I'd been thinking and writing about these birds: Muldoon's trans-Atlantic subjects are the ancestors of those released by Eugene Schiefellin; he moves from the earthbound denizens of an industrial cityscape to the dazzling wheel of birds in flight, all of it hinging upon the lifting of eyes and spirit that comes when you look closely at birds and at the world.

> Indiscernible, for the most part, the welts and weals
> on their two-a-penny skins,
> weals got by tinkering with tin
> foil from condoms or chewing gum, welts as slow to heal
>
> as spot-welds on steel
> in a chop-shop where, by dint of the din,
> their calls will be no clearer than their colors till they spin
> (or are spun) around to reveal
>
> this other sphere in which their hubbub's the hubbub
> of all-night revelers at reveille,
> girls with shoes in hand, boys giving their all
>
> to the sidewalk outside a club,
> their gloom a gloom so distinctly shot through with glee
> they might be dancing still under a disco-ball.

WREN

I N 1926, AS MY ancestor Edward Grey sat down to write *The Charm of Birds*, he was in failing health, near-blind[1] and worn out from decades of political machinating, a tragic war and the many personal losses of a long life. The book is filled with memories, with birdsong, with Grey's love for his first wife, Dorothy, who had died some twenty years earlier. It draws on the time Edward and Dorothy spent together at their cottage in the Itchen Valley, a haven from the demands of politics. 'We made a special life there,' he wrote. 'It was to both of us a lovely refuge. I refused ever to make a political speech within miles of it.' Grey would come here every weekend to immerse himself in nature, in the birds that swarmed around the ramshackle, rose-covered cottage. There are pictures of him with a robin perched on his old tweed cap, another with a mandarin duck eating from his hand.

W.H. Hudson, the great naturalist and one of the few friends to whom the Greys would lend the cottage when they were north at Fallodon[2], described the place as:

> a lodge in the vast wilderness ... pretty well hidden by trees, and [it] has the reed and sedge and grass green valley and swift river before it, and behind on each side green fields and old untrimmed hedges with a few

old oak trees growing both in the hedgerows and the fields ... only the wild birds to keep one company. They knew how to appreciate its shelter and solitariness; they were all about it, and built their nests amid the green masses of honeysuckle, Virginia creeper, rose, and wild clematis which covered the trellised walls and part of the red roof ...

Dorothy, whom Grey married in 1885, kindled her husband's love of birds. While Grey had spent his year after being sent down from Oxford filling the lakes at Fallodon with wildfowl, he was initially more interested in shooting birds than watching them.[3] Dorothy was eccentric, intellectual and a passionate birdwatcher. Reading *The Cottage Book*, a shared journal that the couple kept of their time in Hampshire, which Grey privately published after his wife's death, you get a sense of her leading him deeper into nature, into the lives of the birds that would comfort him when, in 1906, his already sickly wife was thrown from a horse and killed. Grey's biographer, George Macaulay Trevelyan, described Dorothy as 'more in harmony with nature than any human being', while Grey noted in *The Cottage Book* that he 'hardly dare write anything about birds; I am so overshadowed by Dorothy.'

Dorothy shunned the busy political life of London and used to stay at the cottage during the week while Grey was at Parliament. He'd travel down on the last train on a Friday night, or very early Saturday mornings, and they'd spend the weekends watching and listening to birds and noting down their observations. There's a passage in *The Cottage Book*, from April 1894, where Grey writes that he:

came by the last train on Friday night the 27th, and walked out from Winchester at midnight. It was warm and soft: I heard a nightingale, and one sedge warbler was singing within hearing of the road just where a piece of the river could be seen, light at the end of a little dark path. I walked with my hat off and once a little soft rain fell amongst my hair. There were great forms of leafy trees and a smell and spirit everywhere and I felt the soft country dust about my feet.

It was the wren who was the special bird of the cottage and, in *The Charm of Birds*, which Grey wrote in retirement less than a decade before his death, the wren skips and sings across the pages. 'There are individual wren songs that stand up like little peaks of memory,' he writes, recalling Wordsworth.[4] I tell my students that scent is the most memory-filled of the senses, but for Grey it was sound, and *The Charm of Birds* is a hymn to birdsong, to the way he is able to slide down a wren's riotous call to his time at the cottage, to Dorothy. Grey said that one had to be happy to write, but this is a terribly sad book, with Dorothy never mentioned by name, but referred to obliquely as 'one who was with me' or 'a dear friend', as if looking at the loss of her straight-on would snatch away what was left of his sight.[5]

Grey and Dorothy called their favourite walk by the banks of Avington Lake 'Wren Path' because of the number of the birds that sang and nested alongside it. Often when Grey arrived from London he'd walk along the path, checking on the progress of the eggs and fledglings, then stopping to listen to the back and forth choiring: 'when a wren is in good form he sings, as it was said the young Queen Victoria danced at a Court function in Paris, "with decision, and right through to the end."'

One of Dorothy's contributions to *The Cottage Book* speaks of the pleasure that comes from knowing and naming birds: 'The wren sang all morning,' she wrote. 'We talked about it while we were at breakfast, and thought how nice it was that we knew enough to be able to love it so much.' Decades later, in *The Charm of Birds*, Grey recalled coming to the cottage one fine summer's Saturday morning around eight o'clock:

> I had just arrived, and stood in the doorway that opened on to the little lawn . . . in front, some ten yards away, was a poplar tree, and from it a wren sprang into the air, and, singing in an ecstasy as he flew, passed straight over me and over the cottage roof to some other place of bliss on the farther side: 'like a blessing,' said one who was with me.

Max Hastings and Michael Waterhouse have argued fairly conclusively that Grey and Dorothy's relationship was unconsummated – *un marriage blanc*, as Waterhouse phrases it – and that Grey enjoyed any number of metropolitan affairs, producing at least one illegitimate child. Dorothy was his great love, though, and when he writes of birds, it's like she's still at his shoulder, watching the wrens, listening to their immoderate warbling. It's as if all that bird life around them – the nests they fussed over, the stone curlews they lay listening to on the heath, the wrens that frisked in their hedges – became a kind of family for them. This extraordinary closeness comes through on the page – both in *The Cottage Book*, where their words wend together like the roses that tangled over the cottage's trellis, and in *The Charm of Birds*, which is like an elegy for Dorothy, a path back to her across the decades through the voices of the birds. It's enough to change your idea of what love is.

In *Elegy for Jane (My student, thrown by a horse)* Theodore Roethke wrestles with exactly this problem: how to phrase a feeling that doesn't conform to received notions of love. One of his students at the University of Washington, where he was a much-admired teacher of poetry, has died, falling from a horse like Dorothy Grey. The girl is described as:

> A wren, happy, tail into the wind,
> Her song trembling the twigs and small branches.
> The shade sang with her

Roethke's grief is real, and part of his sorrow is the fact that he stands outside of conventional modes of feeling. The poem is a grasping-after of ways to express his sense of loss. The image of the poet-teacher at the girl's funeral in the final stanza is profoundly moving.

> Over this damp grave I speak the words of my love:
> I, with no rights in this matter,
> Neither father nor lover.

Roethke was a keen birdwatcher and Jane is birdlike. Not only is she described as a wren, but also a 'skittery pigeon' and a sparrow. The poet's love for his student won't be pinned down, it flutters away the moment he tries to capture it in traditional phrases of romance or mourning, but there is something liberating in this freedom from convention. Roethke's love for Jane is like a birder's love of birds: complicated, but pure.

There's another melancholy wren in Norman Nicholson's poem about his dead father, 'The Cock's Nest'. A wren begins to build a nest in the poet's garden, the bird's bustling business providing a momentary distraction from the grief, the largeness of empty rooms. But male wrens usually make several nests, leaving some as untenanted decoys, with the female choosing where to lay her eggs.[6]

> They say the cock
> Leases an option of sites and leaves the hen
> To choose which nest she will. She didn't choose our yard.

Spring opens out into summer and the nest is still there, another emptiness. The poem's end is swift and brutal:

> The cock's nest with never a nest in,
> And my father dead.

A wren has been singing outside the boxy, prefab room in which I lecture on Thursday evenings this autumn term, and I stop the class for each burst of song that pours forth from this unlikely-looking maestro: 'the little woodland dwarf, the tiny wren;'[7] 'Nature's DARKLING of this mossy shed',[8] 'an energetic walnut'.[9] The sound is that of the child's toy, shaped like a bird, that is filled with water, blown through with puffed cheeks, and lets out a simulacrum of the wren's unbridled stream of song. It's a moment of beauty, when our wren sings on a Thursday, and my students and I sit back as the babbling spiel of notes drifts in through the open window; in the silence that follows we're often unsure what to say to each other. Hughes describes the wren's voice as 'like a martyr on fire, / Glossolalia'.[10] One of the 'spots in time' in Wordsworth's *The Prelude* is the voice of a wren, heard in childhood:

that single Wren
Which one day sang so sweetly in the Nave
Of the old Church, that, though from recent showers
The earth was comfortless, and, touch'd by faint
Internal breezes, sobbings of the place,
And respirations, from the roofless walls
The shuddering ivy dripp'd large drops, yet still,
So sweetly 'mid the gloom the invisible Bird
Sang to itself, that there I could have made
My dwelling-place, and liv'd for ever there
To hear such music.

One December evening, the last class of term, I abandoned my teaching altogether after a particularly fierce burst of carolling in the frosty late afternoon outside, and gave the students a brief and impromptu lecture on the wren and its literary associations. The bird has an ancient, mythical feel about it, I told them, the students lolling on their desks. Despite Robert Macfarlane describing it as whirring 'from elder bush to elder bush so fast it seems to teleport',[11] the wren feels clockwork and Victorian at the very least, if not snatched from the fabled Britain of Arthur. 'A bird out of Merlin's ear,' Ted Hughes calls him. In *The Book of Merlyn*, the posthumously published conclusion to T.H. White's *The Once and Future King*, the wizard turns Arthur into a white-fronted goose and, flying across the North Sea, the king comes upon a wren hitching a ride on the back of a 'horned owl'. This story reminds us of the fable of the wren and the eagle, where the smaller bird leaped on the back of the larger one in order to fly the highest and prove he was king of the birds. For his cheek, he was consigned to scuttle for scraps in the lowest places, although Hughes infers a more psychological pretext for his earth-hugging flight:

The wren is a nervous wreck
Since he saw the sun from the back of an eagle.
He prefers to creep.[12]

In British and, particularly, Irish folklore, the wren is central to the mummer's play of the wren-boys. The wren must be punished each year for any number of mythical sins: for its hubris in mounting the back of the eagle; for betraying the hiding place of St Stephen to the Sanhedrin, who stoned him to death; for alerting Viking raiders to the presence of hidden Irish soldiers in the 700s. The bird's punishment is to be caught and caged by the wren-boys who, usually on St Stephen's day (26 December), go from door to door begging for coins which they will spend that evening at the wren dance.

I told the students about a book that meant a huge amount to me as a child: *The Dark is Rising* by Susan Cooper. Wren-boys appear during one of the visions into which Will, who is both an eleven-year-old and one of the fabled Old Ones, falls:

> six boys carried a kind of platform made of reeds and branches woven together, with a bunch of holly at each corner. It was like a stretcher, Will thought, except that they were holding it at shoulder height. He thought at first that it was no more than that, and empty; then he saw that it supported something. Something very small. On a cushion of ivy leaves in the centre of the woven bier lay the body of a minute bird: a dusty-brown bird, neat-billed. It was a wren.

Merriman, the book's version of Merlin, explains the scene to Will: 'It is the Hunting of the Wren, performed every year since men can remember, at the solstice,' he says. As Will looks on, the dead bird is transformed into 'the Lady', a fellow Old One who has been guiding Will in his battle against the Dark. It's one of the brilliant moments in the book in which Cooper, an American, seamlessly weaves the deep traditions of British folklore into her storyworld, creating passage after passage that shimmer in the mind.

Wren-boys also turn up in one of Leopold Bloom's fantasies in the Circe chapter of James Joyce's *Ulysses*. Wren was slang for prostitutes in Ireland, and the bird's name comes from the Middle English *wrenne*, meaning lascivious. The symbol of the trapped bird, with its frisky, tumescent little tail, doesn't take much decoding. The boys dance in, chanting the traditional song: 'The wren, the wren, the Lord of all birds, / On St. Stephen's Day was caught on the furze.' Joyce doesn't tell us what happened to the bird in Bloom's dream. In some cases, the wren was put to death, his punishment complete, in others, the bird was freed. Either way, the ritual is about the turning of the year, about the hope of light to come now the darkest day is past.

Carol Ann Duffy's poem, *The Wren-Boys*, brings the ceremony to Bethlehem, telling of a group of wren-boys who can't trap the bird and so fashion a ragged dummy from feathers. The boys, perhaps infected by the wren's proverbial bawdiness, make merry against a mythical backdrop that is part old England, part Holy Land. That spare and surprising last line falls with beautiful solemnity:

> Which would have been news to the wren,
> had it understood claptrap, mythology, fable,
> warm in its communal roost in the stable
> over the heads of the dozing beasts –
>
> while the Wren-Boys boozed and danced at the Inn;
> one with a widow, one with the farmer's daughter,
> one with a sweetheart, one with a sozzled priest.
> Later, the snow settled, a star in the east.

I followed up on this convivial note, sending my students off to their respective festivities, their holiday jobs, their loved ones, with a few lines from *The Christmas Wren* by Gillian Clarke, a kind of companion-piece to Dylan Thomas's *A Child's Christmas in Wales*. It's a story about the joy of the miniature, the pleasure in toys and small things, not least the wren. It starts with a wonderful accordion of images:

> Once there was a house by a lake, and inside it another house – a white farm, its rooms full of waves breaking, and inside the farm a tall red house where at night the foghorn moaned far out at sea like a lost moon. And inside all of them was Christmas.

There follows a little brown bird — a decoration that opens into glorious life at the end of the story. On the top-most branch of the Christmas tree:

> something is quivering, like your heart when you unpack all the Christmases of your life from the box. Something is alive. Something has come in from the snowy dawn. A small brown bird, reflected, again and again, in the glass, as if all the small brown birds in the world were sheltering from the cold on our Christmas tree. On its topmost branch, where the star of Bethlehem should be, quivering, alive, a wren.

SKYLARK

RICHARD JEFFERIES' AUTOBIOGRAPHY, *The Story of My Heart*, tells us almost nothing of its author's short, sad life. It was written in 1883, as the tuberculosis that would kill Jefferies began to show itself in blood-spotted handkerchiefs and digestive complaints. He would live for four more years, long enough to see his third child die of meningitis, long enough to write his mesmerising post-apocalyptic masterpiece, *After London*. He was thirty-eight when he died, the age I will be when these words are published, and he's buried in Broadwater Cemetery, Worthing, not ten minutes' walk from where I grew up, on the rim of land between the chalky South Downs and the sea.

The Story of My Heart is the record of Jefferies' spiritual development, of the way that, through nature, he accessed his 'strong inspiration of soul thought'. It is a lavish, joyful book, some passages coming close to madness, touched perhaps by the *spes phthisica* that is said to induce a kind of euphoria in consumptives. The book is structured as a sequence of recollections in which Jefferies locates himself in a landscape, almost always downland, with the sea in sight, and grass, soft wheat and birds, and through a meditation with the natural world reaches a trembling state of bliss: 'The marvel of existence, almost the terror of it, was flung on me with crushing force by the sea, the sun shining, the distant hills.'

If Jefferies hadn't existed, the downs would have invented him. He's a familiar of those rolling close-cropped hills, at one with the chalk and light and wind. This is the territory of Eric Ravilious and Samuel Palmer, William Blake and W.H. Hudson. Ann Wroe brings all of these figures, and Jefferies, together in her study *Six Facets of Light*, which close-reads the landscape like a poem. 'Aficionados of light and chalk tend,' she says, 'like downland starlings, to flock together.' Wroe notes that Jefferies was enchanted by the 'champagniness' of Sussex light, which 'brings all things into clear relief, giving them an edge and an outline.'

It's not surprising, given his love of the downs and their light, that Jefferies was obsessed with the skylark. 'There is sunshine in the song; the lark and the light are one,' he wrote in *Outdoors in February*, 'and wherever he glides over the wet furrows the glint of the sun goes with him.' One of the more lustrous passages in *The Story of My Heart* sees the author on a grassy hillside, listening to the larks:

> The sun of the summer morning shone on the dome of sward, and the air came softly up from the wheat below, the tips of the grasses swayed as it passed sighing faintly, it ceased, and the bees hummed by to the thyme and heath bells. I became absorbed in the glory of the day, the sunshine, the sweet air, the yellowing corn turning from its sappy green to summer's noon of gold, the lark's song like a waterfall in the sky.

For Jefferies, the lark is part of the constellation of hills, light and wildlife that allows him to speak 'in my soul to the earth, the sun, the air, the distant sea' and, through the lark, Jefferies hears the earth speaking back to him. In a mystical passage in his essay *Wheatfields*, larks seem to overthrow time, so that the birds sing to usher in the summer and winter at once, dawn and dusk concurrently:

> the lark sang again, high in the morning sky. The evenings became dark; still he rose above the shadows and the dusky earth, and his song fell from the bosom of the night. With full untiring choir the joyous host heralded the birth of the corn; the slender forceless seed-leaves which came gently up till they had risen above the proud crests of the lovers.

The skylark is one of the pillars of literary ornithology. In his notebooks, John Clare refers to the bird as 'of as much use in poetry as the nightingale'. It is a particular favourite of the Romantic poets – almost half of my late-Victorian *A Bird-Lover's Anthology* is given over to the skylark: Shelley, Coleridge, Wordsworth and Southey. In her introduction to the *Penguin Book of Bird Poetry*, Peggy Munsterberg points out that the lark, heretofore a 'bird of middling rank', rose to poetic prominence in the eighteenth century – it was anti-allegorical, a bird for the Enlightenment. 'Unlike the bleeding pelican,' she writes, 'which is the essence of the anti-rational, the lark of the poets has always been basically realistic.'

Wordsworth's skylark is typical of the Romantic approach to the bird. It's constitutionally cheerful and 'ne'er could Fancy bend the buoyant Lark / To melancholy service – hark! O hark!' He calls the skylark 'The happiest bird that sprang out of the Ark!' and seems unable to write about it without exclamation marks dotting the page like musical notes. In his 'To a Skylark', he addresses the bird as a:

> Happy, happy Liver!
> With a soul as strong as a mountain River,
> Pouring out praise to the Almighty Giver,
> Joy and jollity be with us both!

There's a uniformity in the emotional register in a skylark's pure and upward-lifting song, and it presents a challenge to writers. Just as some of Jefferies' passages make us wince – 'the deep blue of the unattainable flower of the sky drew my soul towards it' – much of the writing about skylarks is *jejune*, schmaltzy and forgettable. W.H. Hudson wrote that the lark's song was 'sunshine translated into sound', but that sunshine needs shadows in order not to blind us.

This paradox – that the skylark's very joyfulness makes it unknowably other – is at the heart of one of Shelley's greatest poems, 'To a Skylark'. Rather than trying to summon the bird on the page, Shelley wrote a poem about how to write poems about birds. It is the skylark's otherness, Shelley's inability to find metaphors in the language of verse, that energises the writing here and builds towards a fine and complex ending which seeks to accommodate the bird's difference without appropriating it.

Shelley wrote 'To a Skylark' in the summer of 1820, while living at Leghorn. In her note to the poem in my 1872 edition of her late husband's *Collected Works*, Mary Shelley remembers a particular summer evening: 'while wandering among the lanes whose myrtle[1] hedges were the bowers of the fire-flies … we heard the carolling of the skylark which inspired one of the most beautiful of his poems.' 'Hail to thee, blithe Spirit! / Bird thou never wert,' the poem begins, and the bird is 'from Heaven, or near it'. Everything in the poem's opening seeks to distance the skylark from the earth-bound poet and the natural world. It is not a bird, it is a creature made of air and light and song.

> Higher still and higher
> From the earth thou springest
> Like a cloud of fire;
> The blue deep thou wingest,[2]
> And singing still dost soar, and soaring ever singest.

That chiasmus in the final line (from chi, the Greek letter X) mirrors the typical poetic instinct when writing of birds – to effect a crossing over, to situate the poet's consciousness in that of the bird. Instead, Shelley's skylark drifts further and further away, with each attempt to capture it in language doomed to fail. As Harold Bloom says, 'language itself will become an obstacle for defining his "imaginary" skylark.'

> What thou art we know not;
> What is most like thee?
> From rainbow clouds there flow not
> Drops so bright to see
> As from thy presence showers a rain of melody.

There is something heroic in Shelley's attempts to find an analogue for the skylark in staple poetic imagery, as if he and the bird are sparring, the poet seeing all along that his visions of maidens in towers will not be equal to the sublime, unearthly joy of this bird.

Finally, Shelley acknowledges the fundamental artistic difference between the poet and lark: that for humans to appreciate beauty, that beauty must be shadowed by the possibility of loss, and because of this we will never sing with the unthinking blitheness of the skylark. It's a Romantic idea, and a gloomy one, but strikes us here as true, as if it's only by looking closely at the vanishing skylark that we are able to see ourselves:[3]

> We look before and after,
> And pine for what is not:
> Our sincerest laughter
> With some pain is fraught;
> Our sweetest songs are those that tell of saddest thought.

The poet who comes to my mind when I hear a skylark lilting upwards into the air is not Shelley, but John Clare. With Clare (like Jefferies), we feel that part of the poet never leaves the fields of his country childhood, that the birds he writes about are only partially there in the present moment of the poem and exist mainly in memory, in the half-imaginary world of his Helpston youth. Clare's 'The Skylark' opens with a vision of farmland, rendered in iambic pentameter that rolls like the fields: 'Above the russet clods the corn is seen / Sprouting its spiry points of tender green.' Boys roam the landscape, sending up skylarks around them. One of the birds rises:

> with happy wings,
> Winnows the air till in the cloud she sings,
> Then hangs a dust[4] spot in the sunny skies,   .
> And drops and drops till in her nest she lies,

There's also, though, a sense of danger here as the mechanical human world encroaches on Clare's rural idyll. Skylarks nest on the ground, their 'low nest moist with the dews of morn', and are threatened by the ploughs and threshing machines, by the boys on their ramblings. The boys never dream:

That birds which flew so high would drop again
To nest upon the ground where anything
May come at to destroy.

Clare, barely five-foot tall after a malnourished childhood, was a nesting bird himself, and the nests found so frequently in his poems stand for the local, safe and secret places to which he retreated as a young man.[5] He was so firmly ensconced in his home village that when his well-intentioned patron, Earl Fitzwilliam, moved him and his family to a larger cottage in Northborough, scarcely three miles from Helpston, it sparked the onset of the poet's mental breakdown. His career, after the novelty of his 'Northamptonshire peasant poetry' had worn off, took a downward turn, and black moods and delusions befell him until he was sent away to an asylum at High Beach in Essex. He was convinced that he was either Shakespeare or Byron (many of whose poems he re-wrote during his time in the institution) and lived out the last third of his long life cut off from his family, penniless and unknown. 'The Skylark' was published in 1835 in *The Rural Muse*, Clare's fourth and final collection, issued as the poet began his descent into alcoholism and paranoia.

The Rural Muse did not enjoy the success of the earlier volumes, perhaps because poems like 'The Skylark' demonstrated a subtlety and complexity of thought at odds with Clare's reputation as a poet of simple rustic lays. The boys, who had been one of the threats to the skylark's nest, find sudden communion with the bird, who becomes for them (and, as always with Clare, it's tempting to see the poet's younger self in one of the roving boys) a vision of escape from the drudgery and danger of life amongst the rural poor. The boys watch the skylark and wish that they might be:

As free from danger as the heavens are free
From pain and toil, there would they build and be,
And sail about the world to scenes unheard
Of and unseen, – O were they but a bird!

Like Clare, like Jefferies, Isaac Rosenberg was short, weak and in ill-health.[6] He would die at the hands of a sniper on 1 April 1918, just outside Arras. He heard larks as he made his way back across no-man's-land from a mission surveying the Hindenburg Line in early 1918 and wrote 'Returning, We Hear the Larks' that morning, scribbling it on scraps of paper while mired in the mud of the trenches. He mailed the scraps back to his parents in Stepney, who had them published in *Poetry Magazine* after his death. Rosenberg is a great war poet, this one of the great war poems, casting the pet bird of the Romantics against a fallen landswept world. It recognises the ultimate meaninglessness of the birds, how little they care about the men who pin their hopes on mere song. As Carol Rumens put it in an essay in *The Guardian*, 'the poem seems to look into the heart of Romantic epiphany and find an abyss.'

Sombre the night is.
And though we have our lives, we know
What sinister threat lies there.

Dragging these anguished limbs, we only know
This poison blasted track opens on our camp –
On a little safe sleep.

But hark! joy – joy – strange joy.
Lo! heights of night ringing with unseen larks.
Music showering our upturned list'ning faces.

Death could drop from the dark
As easily as song –
But song only dropped,
Like a blind man's dreams on the sand
By dangerous tides,
Like a girl's dark hair for she dreams no ruin lies there,
Or her kisses where a serpent hides.

NIGHTJAR

I N *THE CHARM OF BIRDS*, Edward Grey remembers sitting in a
water-meadow while a nightjar flitted through the falling light around
him. 'The bird was silent till at length in one of its flights it passed quite close
to and saw me.' The scene undergoes a sudden change of register, the gentle
evening rent by the bird's supernatural cry:

> It gave a piercing shriek, such as I had never heard before from any
> bird, and flew straight away out of the meadow. For a moment when
> it discovered me its head had turned in my direction, and the shriek
> seemed to be uttered *at* me. It suggested not so much fear as rage and
> loathing: as if the bird were suddenly aware that, unknown to it, a
> human eye had been watching it, when it believed there was security and
> privacy.

The crepuscular, frog-mouthed nightjar has long been held as a creature of
ill-omen, and it was as if that bird, in a Hampshire meadow at the beginning
of the last century, turned a dark new page in Grey's life.[1] He'd lost Dorothy,
his great love, while the cottage in which they'd been happiest burnt to the
ground. He was named Foreign Secretary and submerged himself in his

work, fighting the Conservatives and belligerent elements within his own Liberal Party as the country lurched towards war. Finally, on 3 August 1914, Grey was informed that Germany had invaded Belgium. That evening, he stood in the Foreign Office with the editor of the *Westminster Gazette*, looking out over St James's Park. 'The lamps are going out all over Europe,' he said. 'We shall not see them lit again in our lifetime.'

The strains of pre-war political life, and the loss of his Hampshire idyll, meant that Grey needed to find new escape routes from London. He headed northwards, first to Fallodon, then to Glen, the vast and gothic home of Eddy and Pamela Tennant in the Scottish Borders. Grey and the Tennants had been friendly for years, but it was only after Dorothy's death that Grey began regularly to journey up to Scotland for long weekends, Christmas and the summer recess.

Pamela Tennant was one of the Wyndham Sisters, daughters of the politician Percy Wyndham, racy, beautiful and promiscuous.[2] It's not known when her affair with Grey began, but Simon Blow, Pamela's great-grandson, suggests that Grey was the father of David Tennant, who was born in 1902 (well before Dorothy's death in 1906).[3] At Glen, Grey found Pamela, but he also found wilderness, fishing, tennis (he'd been five-time British amateur champion in the 1890s) and companionship. One friend he (re)made during his time at Glen was the poet Henry Newbolt, whose rousing Victorian verses and ballyhooing for the war made him amongst the most successful and widely read poets of his day, and mean he is now marooned in history, there on the other side of the trenches, urging doomed youth over the top with poems like 'Vitaï Lampada':[4]

> The river of death has brimmed his banks,
> And England's far, and Honour a name,
> But the voice of a schoolboy rallies the ranks,
> 'Play up! play up! and play the game!'

Newbolt and Grey had been close at Oxford, then drifted apart as Grey discovered Dorothy and politics and Newbolt a career in the law, but at Glen they renewed their friendship over a mutual love of birds and poetry.[5] They went for ornithological rambles in the heather capped hills above the River Tweed, then came back to long dinners, where they'd continue their talk of birds. Newbolt noted in his journal that Grey was happiest when speaking about birds and wondered 'what he manages to talk to other people about while the servants are in the room – birds are a perfect *passe-temps* from the diplomatic point of view.' When the servants were out of the room, the two men might have discussed their unconventional love lives. After Dorothy died, Grey spent more and more time at Glen, until he, Eddy and Pamela lived in an uneasy triangle.[6] Newbolt's set-up was more bizarre, if more openly acknowledged.

When he was twenty-five, Newbolt had fallen in love with Margaret Duckworth, one of a group of poets and aesthetes called the Grecians who gathered around Mary Coleridge. Duckworth was at the time romantically entangled with her cousin, Ella Coltman, a handsome fellow-Grecian. Duckworth agreed to marry Newbolt so long as Ella was included in the relationship. Ella came on honeymoon with them and Henry shared his bed with the women alternately for the next two decades. Susan Chitty notes in *Playing the Game*, her biography of Newbolt, that he kept a strict ledger of the trio's sex life, with ticks against their names that 'represent the number of times he slept with each of his women each month between 1904 and 1917, averaging as much as 12 per head per month.'

Newbolt's most successful nature poem, 'Ode to a Nightjar', records an incident when, early in their married life together, he, Ella and Margaret found a wounded bird on the Duckworth family's Orchardleigh Estate in Somerset.[7] It's a sentimental poem – it's hard to read 'the soul's ocean cave' without a snicker – but the final lines strike powerfully home, when the bird and all other beauty are borne back into the past and fade, as Newbolt's stirring, grandiloquent poems have been blanched by time:

> We loved our nightjar, but she would not stay with us.
> We had found her lying as dead, but soft and warm,
> Under the apple tree beside the old thatched wall.
> Two days we kept her in a basket by the fire,

Fed her, and thought she well might live – till suddenly
In the very moment of most confiding hope
She arised herself all tense, quivered and drooped and died.
Tears sprang into my eyes – why not? The heart of man
Soon sets itself to love a living companion,
The more so if by chance it asks some care of him.
And this one had the kind of loveliness that goes
Far deeper than the optic nerve – full fathom five
To the soul's ocean cave, where Wonder and Reason
Tell their alternate dreams of how the world was made.
So wonderful she was – her wings the wings of night
But powdered here and there with tiny golden clouds
And wave-line markings like sea-ripples on the sand.
O how I wish I might never forget that bird –
Never!
But even now, like all beauty of earth,
She is fading from me into the dusk of Time.

Newbolt's poetic standing never recovered from the war. Like a rock band forced to tour old hits, he was called upon to read from 'Vitaï Lampada' every so often – notably on a visit to Canada in 1923 which attracted large crowds. His new work, though, was ignored or ridiculed, while his love life foundered. Each of the trio took new lovers and the relationship between Henry, Ella and Margaret became one of bitterness and suspicion. Newbolt's poems and prose are now almost entirely out of print.

In *British Birds: their Folklore, Names and Literature*, Francesca Greenoak lists twenty-nine different names for the nightjar and there are dozens more when we consider its American cousins the whip-poor-will and nighthawk.[8] John Clare calls it the fern owl, and his poem of that name conjures the same sense of disquiet that Grey felt as the bird flickered through the lacy dusk around him. Nightjars only churr when they're perching; in flight they're silent, save for the shriek of alarm they utter when startled. Clare writes of the:

fern owl's cry that whews aloft
In circling whirls and often by his head
Wizzes as quick as thought and ill at rest.

Wordsworth finds in the bird's cry 'the spirit of a toil-worn slave, / Lashed out of life, not quiet in the grave.' It is not the cry, but rather the soundlessness of the bird that gives an eerie air to Thomas Hardy's mournful and elegiac 'Afterwards', which imagines how people will speak of the author after his own death. He draws a number of sharply observed portraits of a natural world flourishing when he is gone, including a glimpse of a 'dewfell-hawk', which Mark Cocker and Richard Mabey suggest comes from reading a description of a nightjar in one of John Clare's letters: 'they make an odd noise in the evening, beginning at dewfall . . . '

in the dusk when, like an eyelid's soundless blink,
The dewfall-hawk comes crossing the shades to alight
Upon the wind-warped upland thorn

Hardy was seventy-seven when he published the poem, not expecting to live much longer – it was a leave-taking, and was read at his memorial service ten years later. The critic Merryn Williams noted that it seemed that Hardy wished to be remembered 'not as a poet or a novelist, but simply as a loving observer of nature', In my Oxford World Classics copy of Hardy's poems, edited by my grandfather, Samuel Hynes, the poem is covered in my untidy annotations, the dewfall-hawk circled twice. I read it as a teenager, with an adolescent's interest in death, and yet it was not the poem's funereal aspect, but rather the blitheness with which Hardy addresses the subject of his own demise that fascinated me. The nightjar has ever since seemed to me to live a half-life caught between our world and a chthonic netherworld, where he churrs amid the shades and shadows.

The nightjar's cry sends J.A. Baker off into raptures in *The Peregrine*.[9] Early on in the book, we find the following passage, which, even though it's not about Baker's beloved falcon, is somehow emblematic of the bonkers brilliance of his prose:

> The first bird I searched for was the nightjar, which used to nest in the valley. Its song is like the sound of a stream of wine spilling from a height into a deep and booming cask.[10] It is an odorous sound, with a bouquet that rises to the quiet sky. In the glare of day it would seem thinner and drier, but dusk mellows it and gives it vintage. If a song could smell, this song would smell of crushed grapes and almonds and dark wood. The sound spills out, and none of it is lost. The whole wood brims with it. Then it stops. Suddenly, unexpectedly. But the ear hears it still, a prolonged and fading echo, draining and winding out among the surrounding trees.

It's that echo, the whirring, winding song, that thrums at the end of Joanna Newsom's *Time, As a Symptom*, the last track on her album, *Divers*, which constructs a kind of Benjaminian constellation where past, present and future overlap. The nightjar is one of the birds that flits across the album. Newsom's heroic soldiers Rufus Nightjar and Private Poorwill appear and reappear on different battlefields in different centuries, until the last song, when they're in space, spiralling out into the void, and the repeated final lines knit time into a circle.

> White star, white ship—Nightjar, transmit: transcend!
> White star, white ship—Nightjar, transmit: transcend!
> White star, white ship—Nightjar, transmit: trans . . .[11]

SWIFT

W HEN I WAS EIGHTEEN I moved to Paris to live in the attic rooms of a grand Quai d'Orsay apartment block. I had come to spend a year with my godmother, who was in the depths of a terrible depression. I arrived in late August to find my godmother confined to her vast golden bed and, up there in the smudgy heights, swifts were my only companions. I'd sit at my dormer window looking out over the Seine, reading, enjoying the loneliness, and looking up to see the birds boomerang high over the water. I thought of Edward Thomas's 'Haymaking', where he wrote of how:

> shrill shrieked in his fierce glee
> The swift with wings and tail as sharp and narrow
> As if the bow had flown off with the arrow.

I, barely out of the nest myself, watched the dusky fledglings absurdly confident on their new-made wings. I felt a fraternal interest in them, thinking of their arduous journey ahead, of the heights and miles they'd fly. As the evening light faded over canted zinc roofs, I'd put my book aside, rest my chin on my hands on the window-frame and look out at the swifts. Their shrieks soundtracked my evenings – kids on aerial rollercoasters. When, a decade and a half later, I read Robert MacFarlane on the joy of watching swifts, I was swept right back there to my attic room, moored in the Parisian sky.

> Above me, swifts hunted the dusk air over the scarp slope. They turned so sharply and smoothly and at such speed that it seemed the air must be honeycombed with transparent tubes down which the swifts were sliding, for surely nothing else could account for the compressed control of their turns.[1]

Swifts give us access to another mode of being, Macfarlane suggests, opening up the translucent landscapes of the air.

> Their flight-paths lent contour to the sky and their routes outlined the berms and valleys of wind which formed and re-formed at that height, so that the air appeared to possess a topology of its own, made visible by the birds' motion.[2]

There is a hierarchy to the skies and at the apex is the swift. We look up through time-shared air with its layers of birds, from the hedge-dwellers and the tree-perchers to the crows and finches of the lower air, through the strata of gulls and migrating geese and wading birds, to the swifts on their vectors through the stratosphere. Gilbert White wasn't known as a poet, but the sight of the birds above his Hampshire church in the warm May of 1769 moved him to verse:

> Mark the swift in rapid giddy ring
> Dash round the steeple, unsubdued of wing;
> Amusive birds!

Swifts live and sleep and mate on the wing, only coming down to earth to build their nests, which are formed of flotsam — threads, leaves, spider-webs, feathers — and whatever they can snatch from the air. Anne Stevenson's 'Swifts' fully captures the splendour of looking up into a swift-sickled sky.

bolt nocks bow to carry one sky-scyther
Two hundred miles an hour across fullblown windfields.
Swereee swereee. Another. And another.
It's the cut air falling in shrieks on our chimneys and roofs.

Stevenson names them 'air pilgrims, pilots of air rivers;' 'they outfly storms,' she says, they 'rush to the pillars of altitude, the thermal fountains.' Then, a moment of stillness in the poem's careening breathlessness. When night falls, the swifts are 'Sleepers over oceans in the mill of the world's breathing.'

The thought of the birds sleeping on the wing moved something in Annie Dillard as she watched them wheeling over the waters of the Holy Land. 'I saw swifts mate in midair,' she writes in *For the Time Being*. 'At Kibbutz Lavi, in the wide-open hills above the Sea of Galilee, three hundred feet above me under the sky, the two swifts flew together in swoops, falling and catching.' If you have ever watched swifts mate, you'll know the shiver of that brief, wind-whipped cloacal kiss. 'How do birds mate in midair?' Dillard asks, before going on to describe, with what Robert Lowell calls 'the grace of accuracy', what she sees:

> They start high. Their beating wings tilt them awkwardly sometimes and part those tiny places where they join, often one of the pair stops flying and they lose altitude ... Alone they rise fast, tensely, until you see only motes that chase, meet – you, there, here, out of all this air! – and spiral down; breaks your heart. At dusk, I learned later, they climb so high that at night they actually sleep in the air.

The swift is the most airborne of birds, and you feel that if they could fashion nests up there in the mare's tale cirrus clouds, they would. They drift up into unknown reaches and they take our wonder with them. In a remarkable book, *Being a Beast*, Charles Foster goes further, trying to become a swift. Having in earlier chapters hitched his consciousness to a badger and an otter, he recognises that the swift represents the greatest challenge to his sympathetic imagination. 'Swifts are the ultimate other,' he says. 'As fast as thought, though bolder . . . thought cannot snatch the blueness of the height or know that the whole life of each swift is a gasp.'[3]

When you live with swifts, they give shape to your world. A swift hatches in the roof of Foster's Oxford home:

> It came back the following summer, circled our house, didn't breed, went again, again and again to Africa, came back to Oxford and then found a hole in the house and a home for its semen. Until it flew into our roof above my head, it hadn't touched the ground, or a tree, or a building, or anything but insects and the air in four years.

It's a sublime thought. 'It's not surprising that poets get all ethereal about swifts. If anything can be literally ethereal, swifts are,' Foster says. Our ancestors seemed to find something disquieting about the birds – in *Birds Britannica* Mark Cocker and Richard Mabey list the bird's historical names: 'devil's bitch', 'deviling', 'devil', 'devil bird', 'skeer devil', 'screecher', 'screamer' and 'shriek owl'. Foster, though, reaches for a metaphor on the side of the light, recognising the futility of his mission to enter into any kind of communion with the birds, and seeing a kind of glory in it: 'becoming a swift? I might as well try to be God.'

Foster's book is very good on the losses that come with the end of summer, foremost amongst them the departure of the swifts, who are with us for barely a quarter of the year. 'When they left I couldn't bear it,' he writes. In *Nature Cure*, Richard Mabey suffers the opposite problem. The swifts have been a totemic bird for him growing up. His indifference to the 'careering midsummer silhouettes' of swifts is the first sign of the depression that will come to swamp him. 'I was blind to the swifts for the first time in my life. While they were *en fête* I was lying on my bed with my face away from the window, not really caring if I saw them again or not.'[4]

The sense of anomie that replaces his usual euphoria at the arrival of the swifts sends Mabey back to an earlier encounter with a bird, this time in the Cevennes, that came to seem like a premonition of the dark days that lay ahead (and the foretaste of an eventual, miraculous, recovery). He came across a 'fledgling swift beached in the attic' of the farmhouse he was sharing with friends. He picked it up, noting its claws 'mounted on little more than feathered stumps', and hurled it from the window. 'It went into a downward slide, winnowing furiously, skimmed so close to the road that we all gasped, and then flew up strongly towards the south-east. It would not touch down again until it came back to breed in two summers' time.'

This passage recalls 'Swifts', a poem by Ted Hughes in which he too finds a stranded fledgling, although the ending this time is less fortunate. The poet tosses the bird into the air, only to see it crash down amongst the raspberry canes. He takes it indoors and tries to feed it: 'The moustached goblin savage / Nested in a scarf.' Eventually, exiled from the life-giving air, the swift dies.

> The inevitable balsa death.
> Finally burial
> For the husk
> Of my little Apollo

Like Mabey, like Hughes, the botanist William Herbert (1778–1847) found a stricken swift and attempted to nurse it back to health. There's something about the image of these big, broken men cupping the beached birds in their palms that is terribly moving. Herbert was the third son of the Earl of Carnarvon, a politician and lawyer who, at the age of thirty-four, took holy orders and became a naturalist clergyman in the mould of his hero, Gilbert White. In his (somewhat over-extensive) notes to White's *The Natural History of Selbourne*, Herbert writes that one July in the 1820s he 'observed some children tossing up a full grown young swift which could not fly, and had fallen down from its nest in the lofty tower of the church.' He took the bird home and fed it 'a little meal and hard egg mixed with bread, and a good deal of finely sifted fig dust.' Herbert kept the swift in a cage formed of piled books – one of them Johnson's *Dictionary* – and slowly trained it to fly again.

The end of August came and the swifts above Herbert's West Riding parsonage were beginning to depart. 'I had carried it through two or three rooms lying on the palm of my hand,' Herbert writes, 'and was in the act of stroking its head with my fingers, when, upon the swifts screaming in the air, it suddenly sprang out of my hand and flew low round the carriage drive.' The bird made one final fly-by, as if to bid farewell to its saviour:

> Passing over my head as it came round, it rose high in the air to join the wild swifts, and was never seen by us again. Three days after, the swifts had all departed; and I make little doubt that in less than a week after its vain attempts to surmount Johnson's *Dictionary*, my young friend was flying sky high in the heart of Africa. I know nothing more marvellous, than such an abrupt transition from a state of the most imbecile hopelessness and sloth, to such ethereal activity.

I remember how sad I was when the swifts left my Parisian eyrie, how much I missed their screeching when, in the evening, I'd return home and sit at the window watching *bateaux-mouches* chugging mournfully past, looking out over the cascading grey roofs towards Montmartre. Those swifts were the only birds in Paris, or so it seemed to me, and the sky was empty without them.

When the birds came back, nine months later, I was in love with a French-Vietnamese girl – her face as sharp and triangular as a swift's – who lived on the Rue de la Roquette. I'd often walk back across Paris in the day's first light, over the unpeopled Place de la Bastille then down to the river, following the trail of swifts casting for insects above the Seine, all the way to my apartment, where their busy screeching filled the air. Paris seemed Paris again with the birds there. I still have a copy of Hughes's *New and Selected Poems* with a *Shakespeare and Company – Kilometer Zero, Paris* stamp inside it, and I turned repeatedly to his 'Swifts' that year, copying into my orange Rhodia notebook this celebration of the annual relief we feel when the swifts drop in from their African homes.

> They've made it again,
> Which means the globe's still working, the Creation's

Still waking refreshed, our summer's
Still all to come –
      And here they are, here they are again
Erupting across yard stones
Shrapnel-scatter terror.

When I left Paris, my godmother better and student life calling, the swifts were still there. On my last evening I sat at the window, alone again (the swift-faced girl had dumped me) and watched the birds scything the air above the river, 'screaming parties racing in the half-light', as William Fiennes calls them.[5] 'Swifts lay open the sky so that we can go there,' Charles Foster writes. 'They slash the veil.'[6] I was out there with them, fixing in the amber of memory that skyline, that light, those birds.

I was leaving Paris for Oxford where, in an early manuscript version of D.H. Lawrence's *Sons and Lovers*, read in the Radcliffe Camera at dusk, I'd find a passage that seemed like a message from my swifts above the Seine. I copied it into the same orange notebook as the Hughes poem. In it, Mrs Morel stands in the garden of 'the Bottoms', wishing to:

> look at the flowers and to breathe the evening . . . So she was alone. The
> black swifts, that the children called 'devilins,' darted to and fro like
> black arrow-heads just above her, veering round the corner of the house,
> flying in at the broad eaves, then slipping out again and darting down the
> air with little cries, that seemed to come out of the light, not from the
> noiseless birds.

PEACOCK

FROM THE CANOPIED BED in which my father-in-law died, I can hear peacocks yowling from the grounds of the Victorian mansion next door. It's a dreary-looking, red-brick building, bristling with spires and crenelations, and the peacocks strut its terraces like sentries, rattling their tails importantly with ringing calls.[1] It's September and my wife is still downstairs in the drawing room of the Shropshire farmhouse in which she was raised. I, though, have come up early to lie in bed and listen to the peacocks, to picture them in my half-dreaming mind, their tails 'full of fierce planets with eyes that were each ringed in green and set against a sun that was gold in one second's light and salmon-colored in the next.'[2]

The peacocks give out a high, mournful '*may-awe*!' as Raymond Carver hears it, 'a discordant row of selfishness triumphant' according to D.H. Lawrence or, for Flannery O'Connor, who kept peacocks for most of her life:

> *Lee-yon lee-yon,*
> *Mee-yon mee-yon!*
> *Eee-e-yoy eee-e-yoy,*
> *Eee-e-yoy eee-e-yoy!*

The sound, just as I'm dropping off to sleep, calls up other peacocks: on the lush lawns of Indian hotels; in the garden of Mini, my goddaughter in Holland Park; in the grounds of an Oxfordshire stately home where, at nineteen, I lay in bed with a girl and told her that one day I'd have terraces on which peacocks would strut and furl their lustrous tails. I even quoted Cowper at her:

> That self-applauding bird, the peacock, see;
> Mark what a sumptuous pharisee is he!
> Meridian sunbeams tempt him to unfold
> His radiant glories, azure, green, and gold;

I arrived at Oxford with only the vaguest idea of who I might be and fell quickly into that glib *Brideshead* fantasy, so easy to embrace, with its template for life amid the dreaming spires. I began to speak without moving my jaw and played up my grand ancestors and admitted little of my unglamorous, birdwatching childhood. My university years were catastrophic, really, redeemed only by the few friends who saw through me, by three decent, patient teachers – Tom Paulin, Emma Smith and Charlotte Brewer – and by Henry Green, whom I discovered in my first year and still read and love as deeply nearly twenty years later, sliding down his words into the shoes of that preening peacock of a boy, sprawled on the steps of the Sheldonian, all white tie and champagne.

Loving is Green's masterpiece, and was pressed on me by my grandfather when I was down in Hampstead during my first term at Oxford. I'd brought along my then-girlfriend, the daughter of a Tory MP, and we stopped off at Keith Fawkes on Flask Walk, one of my favourite bookshops. My grandfather bought me the Penguin paperback of *Loving* that I still have, its spine now held together with Sellotape that shatters when you touch it, its pages deckled with re-reading. He told us he was jealous of the two of us, that we had all of Henry Green ahead.

Loving is set during the Second World War at Kinalty Castle in Ireland. Its English owner, Mrs Tennant, is vague and widowed and often absent.

In her place, we find the reduced ranks of largely English staff who manage the estate, where money is tight and the threat of Irish Republicanism all around. The old butler, Eldon, has just died and the wheedling, Steerpike-like Charley Raunce has taken his place. In a *Paris Review* interview, Green said that he:

> got the idea of Loving from a manservant in the Fire Service during the war. He was serving with me in the ranks, and he told me he had once asked the elderly butler who was over him what the old boy most liked in the world. The reply was: 'Lying in bed on a summer morning, with the window open, listening to the church bells, eating buttered toast with cunty fingers.' I saw the book in a flash.

Sebastian Faulks writes of the 'ubiquitous peacocks' of the novel, and they are indeed everywhere at Kinalty, kept with obsessive pride by the only Irishman below stairs, O'Connor. The peacocks are a symbol of the English ascendency's self-regard, a relic of the pomp and luxury that now has no place in rebellious, ramshackle Ireland. A dead, maggot-infested peacock is hung in the castle's outside larder: the state of Anglo-Irish relations. Edith, a housekeeper, used to wear the birds' feathers in her hair in happier times. Now when her lover, Charley, offers her one, she looks puzzled. 'Whatever should I do with one of those?' she asks. Instead, she steals peacock eggs and sells them to supplement her meagre wages.

The cries of the peacocks intensify – 'shriek upon far shriek' – as Mrs Tennant and her daughter-in-law come back to inspect the gothic pile with its closed-up, dusty rooms. The birds' voices are at once a warning and a lamentation – all of this is about to be swept into the past. At the end of the novel, though, we are left with a moving picture of Charley and Edith amongst the birds, about to set off for a new life together in England:

> She began to feed the peacocks. They came forward until they had her surrounded. Then a company of doves flew down on the seat to be fed. They settled all over her. And their fluttering disturbed Raunce who

reopened his eyes. What he saw then he watched so that it could be guessed that he was in pain with his great delight. For what with the peacocks bowing at her purple skirts, the white doves nodding on her shoulders round her brilliant cheeks and her great eyes that blinked tears of happiness, it made a picture.

I couldn't abide D.H. Lawrence when I first came across him at Oxford, not so long after I'd discovered Henry Green. *The White Peacock*, his first, flawed, novel, was written when he was twenty, the age at which I read it. Returning now to my densely-annotated university copy, I can see why I took so ferociously against him. The great critic Barbara Hardy cited Cyril's first-person narrative as 'the model of how not to do it', while Lawrence himself called the book 'nine-tenths adjectives . . . altogether a sloppy, spicy mess'.[3] The plot is non-existent, the characters mere pegs to hang opinions upon. I've only come to love Lawrence by putting aside his novels altogether and re-imagining him solely as a poet and writer of short stories.

In 'Wintry Peacock' from Lawrence's *England, My England*, the narrator, a stand-in for Lawrence in all but name, goes back to Tible, the village in which he'd grown up, and meets a woman outside a cow-shed. Her name is Mrs Goyte and she has come down in the world, marrying a local lad, Alfred, who's been off fighting in France. Three peacocks brought over from her parents' grand home follow Mrs Goyte around; one of them, Joey, putting his head in her lap while she fawns over him. It's a story in which there is nothing hopeful or virtuous. The narrator conspires with Alfred, who has had a love-child in France, to deceive Mrs Goyte, and Joey the peacock is a symbol of the corruption and squalor of these little lives, of all Mrs Goyte's frustrated ambition.

It's no coincidence, I think, that the peacock in Raymond Carver's story, 'Feathers', is also called Joey. In some ways it's a re-writing of 'Wintry Peacock', transplanted to small-town America, but this time the peacock goes through a subtle transformation. Joey belongs to Bud and Olla, a couple who live down 'winding little roads' past 'pastures, rail fences, milk cows moving slowly towards old barns.' As the narrator and his wife, Fran, who have been invited for dinner, go up the steps to the house, they are startled by a peacock, which, like Mrs Goyte's Joey, is a faithful pet. 'Damn bird doesn't know it's a bird, that's its major trouble,' Bud says.

Through the eyes of the narrator, we look askance at the tumbledown house and its eccentric inhabitants. But the more time we spend with Olla, Bud and their monstrous baby, Harold, the more we, and the narrator, come to appreciate the love between them. Bud has paid for Olla to have her teeth fixed and the mould for her dentures sits on top of the television. Joey the peacock is another emblem of Bud's love for his wife. She tells the narrator that she 'always dreamed of having me a peacock. Since I was a girl and found a picture in a magazine. I thought it was the most beautiful thing I'd ever seen. I cut that picture out and put it over my bed.'

Joey's aristocratic finery is out of place in the down-at-heel little house next to the dentures and the huge, ugly baby, but Carver, unlike Lawrence, doesn't punish his characters for their pretensions. We realise that Bud is proud of Harold and loves Joey – 'You can see why they call them birds of paradise,' he says when the peacock is let into the house after dinner. It is the narrator and Fran who come to suffer, with the image of the peacock and the baby and the tight, dignified love of Bud and Olla somehow managing to eat away at whatever there was between them. The ending is restrained and heartbreaking, with the narrator thinking back to the moment they'd left Bud's house and Olla had handed Fran a bunch of peacock feathers, as if wishing to pass on some part of their happiness.

W.B. Yeats and Ezra Pound lived together at Stone Cottage, near Coleman's Hatch in Ashdown Forest, for three winters at the beginning of the First World War. Pound, at twenty-eight, was two decades younger than Yeats, and ostensibly the older man's secretary. The poets retreated from London to work and talk, walking out after dinner to drink cider at the village pub. 'At night,' wrote Yeats,

> when the clouds are not too dark and heavy, a great heath is beautiful with a beauty that is not distracting. One comes in full of thoughts.

> When I am in the country like this I find that life grows more and more
> exciting till at last one is wretched when one goes back to London.

In *Pisan Cantos*, Pound remembers the closely confined lives they led in the cottage, as he worked upstairs and Yeats declaimed below:

> I recalled the noise in the chimney as it were the wind in the chimney but
>   was in reality Uncle William
> downstairs composing
> that he had made a great Peeeeacock
> in the proide ov his oiye
> had made a great peeeeeeecock in the ... made a great peacock
> in the proide of his oyyee
> as indeed he had, perdurable

Yeats's composition would eventually work itself into the poem 'Me Peacock', which Pound published in *Modern Poetry* in May 1914. Yeats had written the poem the previous November, and it was probably inspired by an unusual lunch that was being planned at that time.

'On 18 January 1914, seven poets gathered to eat a peacock,' Lucy McDiarmid, one of my grandfather's old students, writes in *The Peacock Dinner*, her record of the meal that Pound and Yeats gave for Wilfrid Scawen Blunt. Blunt, a now-forgotten late-Romantic poet, was married to Byron's granddaughter and was 'the grandest of old men, the last of the great Victorians'. He had gone to prison for championing Irish nationalism and had lived a vivid, peripatetic life, breeding horses in Egypt and writing fierce poetry against the establishment. Pound and Yeats's lunch for him, which was attended by Hilaire Belloc and Richard Aldington, amongst others, was a whole roast peacock.[4] The bird was Lady Gregory's idea, and the peacock was enjoyed in its full symbolic weight, both as a tribute to the grand old poet in his stately home with its medieval fallalery and as a sign of the coming of a new order. The eating of the peacock represented the overturning of Blunt's Victorian age, with its prissy aestheticism and Orientalism, and the arrival of the Modernists with their battle-cry of 'make it new'. Blunt, who dismissed modernism as 'word games' and looks frankly baffled in the photographs of the lunch, was feasting at his own artistic funeral, a man who 'has made a great peacock / With the pride of his eye.'

GOLDFINCH

OVER THE ROAD FROM the Serpentine Gallery, and not far from where I used to live on a cul-de-sac in Notting Hill, there's a bird sanctuary. In the borderlands between Kensington Gardens and Hyde Park, enclosed by a high yew hedge, a stone memorial stands, a still place in London's back garden. All around, there are bird feeders where greenfinches and sparrows yammer. Blackbirds and wrens skulk and trill in the bushes. Charms of goldfinches, those connoisseurs, have made the niger seed feeder their own, and rise from it in a cloud of red and gold when you enter the enclave, 'like something ceremonial and Japanese,' Jonathan Franzen says in *The New Yorker*.[1] Then they return, guardedly, as you lean your bicycle against the bench and sit down by the wrought-iron fence, overlooking the green waters of the pond.

The memorial is called *Rima* and was designed by Jacob Epstein, the lettering by Eric Gill. In Portland Stone the colour of winter clouds, it shows a naked young woman surrounded by birds, her hair flying out in the breeze. It caused a stir when unveiled by Prime Minister Stanley Baldwin in 1925 — the *Daily Mail* urged the government to 'get this horror out of our park'. The memorial is to the British/Argentinian author and naturalist W.H. Hudson, and I'd often stop there on my way to work in the mornings or in the evenings, just as dusk was falling. I was unhappy in my job, you see, making money when I should have been making words, and they gave me strength, those few minutes snatched from the day. When I was feeling particularly wretched at my desk, as if my life had boarded the wrong bus, I'd remember the goldfinches, the time spent with the spirit of Hudson.

I'd only read a couple of Hudson's novels back then – *Green Mansions* and *A Crystal Age*. Rima is from the first of these, a wild girl of the forest who leads the hero through the Amazon and towards a deeper communion with nature. Since then, I've read everything by Hudson I could get my hands on, as well as the intimate and revealing quasi-biography by Jason Wilson, *Living in the Sound of the Wind*.[2] Hudson comes across as charming, eccentric, desperate, with a sense of the boy, running wild on the Pampas, trapped within the London man.

Hudson's memoir of his Argentinian youth, *Far Away and Long Ago*, is a cracking book, describing in shimmering language the light and air of the Pampas, the wattle-and-daub hut in which he was born, the sense of a childhood pressed close-up against the natural world. The memoir ends – tragically – with the bout of rheumatic fever that killed his mother and left him with chest problems for the rest of his life.[3] After this, Hudson worked as a shepherd, then in the Argentinian national guard, fighting in the Paraguayan Wars. By the time he sailed for England in the late 1860s, Hudson, known as Guillermo Enrique, had collected over 500 bird specimens for the Smithsonian Museum in Washington.[4]

Hudson's writing on birds is immaculate, the quality of the prose exquisite. It's easy to see why he and Edward Grey were such close friends. Hudson was the only person permitted to use the Greys' Hampshire cottage when they were away. This may have stemmed as much from charity as friendship, though. While Hudson's Kensington and Bayswater addresses may sound grand to us now, his was a precarious and shiftless existence until Grey secured him a Civil Service pension in 1901, when Hudson was sixty. It is said that the memorial in Hyde Park stands on the spot where Hudson used to sleep rough during his early years in London. It's likely, though, that he was just birdwatching, as this passage in *Birds in London* about sleeping on the roof of his Kensington Gardens home in November suggests:

At this mutable season a person who elects to spend his nights on the
roof, with rugs and an umbrella to keep out the cold and wet, may
be rewarded by hearing far-off shrill delicate noises of straggling
sandpipers or other shore birds on passage, or the mysterious cry of the
lapwing wailing his way from cloud to cloud.

Goldfinches appear in a poem I studied at school – 'The Great Hunger' by
Patrick Kavanagh. It tells of an Ireland:

Where the potato-gatherers like mechanised scarecrows move
Along the side-fall of the hill ... Here crows gabble over worms and frogs
And the gulls like old newspapers are blown clear of the hedges, luckily.

There's little to redeem these grim lives of grubby toil, although, occasionally, nature will offer some small solace:

The goldfinches on the railway paling were worth looking at –
A man might imagine then
Himself in Brazil and these birds the birds of paradise
And the Amazon and the romance traced on the school map
    lived again.

It was perhaps because of their exoticism that Hudson loved goldfinches so
much – envoys from his gaudy childhood. He returns again and again in his
writing to 'this most charming and most persecuted of all small birds', which
had been driven to near-extinction by its popularity as a caged pet. There's
a wonderful passage in *Adventures with Birds* where the young Guillermo
remembers trapping goldfinches as a child:

I had no binocular and didn't even know that such an instrument
existed; and at last to satisfy the craving I took it into my head to catch
them — to fill my hands with goldfinches and have them in numbers.

He remembers that he'd wanted 'to look at a goldfinch as I would look at a flower.' But the pleasure soon turned to sadness, as 'the terror and distress of my little captives, and their senseless frantic efforts to get out of their prison, began to annoy and make me miserable.' He set the birds free and felt his spirits lift with them.[5]

For the wandering, impoverished Hudson, who liked to stride across the Downs because the wind in his face reminded him of the Pampas, Argentina was always present in his English ramblings. He writes of being at Ryme Intrinseca in Dorset, a place he'd visited only because he liked the name, which asserts a strange hold on him – 'the pretty name of that village makes me reluctant to leave it.' In the empty and overgrown churchyard, he comes upon a flock of 'goldfinches, the little company of twelve fluttering with anxious cries about my head, a very charming spectacle'. The birds summon for Hudson a powerful vision, such that his childhood self almost seems to visit him amongst the gravestones:

> We are familiar with the powerful emotional effect of certain odours, associated with our early life, in this connection; occasionally effects equally strong are produced by sights and sounds, and this was one. As I stood in the churchyard watching the small flutterers in their black and gold and crimson liveries, listening to their excited cries, a vision of my boyhood was brought before me, so vivid as to seem like reality. After many years I was a boy once more, in my own distant home, and the time was October, when the brilliant spring merges into hot summer. I was among the wind-rustled tall Lombardy poplars, inhaling their delicious smell, at that spot where a colony of a couple of dozen black-headed siskins were breeding ... They are now fluttering about me, like these of Ryme Intrinseca, displaying their golden feathers in the brilliant sunshine, uttering their agitated cries ...

Hudson, one of the founders of the RSPB, played a central role in securing protected status for the goldfinch in Britain. Thanks to his efforts and numerous, rather *de haut en bas* letters, hunting and trapping the bird was banned almost everywhere by 1910. Thomas Hardy was a strident campaigner against the Flemish practice of *Vinkensport*: blinding songbirds to encourage them to sing more sweetly. His poem 'The Caged Goldfinch' appeared next to 'The Blinded Bird' in his 1913 collection *Moments of Vision*. It's a short, ghostly piece: the doomed bird left in tribute by an unknown hand.[6]

> Within a churchyard, on a recent grave,
> I saw a little cage
> That jailed a goldfinch. All was silence save
> Its hops from stage to stage.
> There was inquiry in its wistful eye,
> And once it tried to sing;
> Of him or her who placed it there, and why,
> No one knew anything.

Hardy's poem summons the radiance of a painting. Goldfinches have always featured in religious art, their fondness for thistles linked to Christ and his crown of thorns. When I hear 'goldfinch', part of me sees the chipper little bird that flocks around the thistle-bush outside my library door, the one so perfectly captured by Keats in 'I Stood Tip-Toe Upon a Little Hill':

> one by one will drop
> From low hung branches; little space they stop;
> But sip, and twitter, and their feathers sleek;
> Then off at once, as in a wanton freak:
> Or perhaps, to show their black, and golden wings
> Pausing upon their yellow flutterings.

Another part of my goldfinch is kept in a galleried upper corridor of the Uffizi, high above the umber waters of the Arno. Bronzino's *Portrait of Giovanni de' Medici as a Child holding a Goldfinch* shows a ruddy little two-year-old clasping a goldfinch in pudgy fingers against the pink doublet.

The man young Giovanni will become is already detectible in the flushed cheeks, the wisps of golden hair.[7] A few rooms deeper into the museum hangs the *Madonna del Cardellino* by Raphael. John the Baptist, just a child, plump and tousled like Giovanni de' Medici, is holding a goldfinch which the infant Christ, unsteady on his legs, reaches out to stroke. Mary is behind them, the red of her tunic precisely the red of the goldfinch's head. Jesus's foot, touchingly, is placed on top of his mother's, as if she might help him to walk.

It's a painting of a goldfinch, by Carel Fabritius, that acts as the McGuffin in Donna Tartt's *The Goldfinch*.[8] Theo, our hero, is visiting the Metropolitan Museum of Art with his mother. They are standing in front of Fabritius's painting, which is Theo's mother's favourite.[9] Theo notes that:

> It was a direct and matter-of-fact little creature, with nothing sentimental about it; and something about the neat, compact way it tucked down inside itself—its brightness, its alert watchful expression—made me think of pictures I'd seen of my mother when she was small: a dark-capped finch with steady eyes.

A bomb goes off, the mother is killed, Theo takes the painting and its unrealisable yet astronomical value, its great beauty, its manifold symbolisms: all propel the narrative towards its fiery finish.

I'll end though, with a less stylised bird, and a free one. Edward Thomas, like John Clare, seemed to have a visionary and incantatory way with birds. In 'The Hollow Wood', one of his best, Thomas uses the relentless joy of the goldfinch to bring out the gloomy, lifeless wood beneath. The 'twit' in the second line is both the bird's call and perhaps Thomas's opinion of the goldfinch, who can manage to be so blithe when all below is dying. In the end, though, the bird seems to win out, a creature of the sun, set apart from the ominous fish-like birds that swim beneath him.

Out in the sun the goldfinch flits
Along the thistle-tops, flits and twits

Above the hollow wood
Where birds swim like fish –
Fish that laugh and shriek –
To and fro, far below
In the pale hollow wood.

Lichen, ivy, and moss
Keep evergreen the trees
That stand half-flayed and dying,
And the dead trees on their knees
In dog's-mercury, ivy, and moss:
And the bright twit of the goldfinch drops
Down there as he flits on thistle-tops.

ROBIN

W E WERE MARRIED IN December, by candlelight, and came down the aisle to 'Hark the Herald Angels Sing'. Our friend Nikki read of the nativity, the shepherds and the wise men (my grandfather recited Michael Longley's 'Epithalamion'); then, in the flickering light, a Welsh Male Voice Choir sang high and sad, making even the Christmas carols we'd chosen sound forlorn. The Shropshire wind blew hard against the homely little Victorian church, and the figures in the crèche in the transept appeared to huddle closer around the glowing manger, with its plastic Christ, as the candles shuddered.

We were ferried from the church to my mother-in-law's, where a marquee had been hitched between the house and the stables, and two dozen Christmas trees arranged to form a winter forest, amongst which were tables, a jazz band and dancing. The trees were hung with tinsel and baubles and, on almost every branch, a stuffed owl or robin perched. By 2 a.m., when Father Christmas arrived with a fur-piled sleigh to whisk us away, people were dancing barefoot on a chessboard floor bright with broken glass. A couple were making love in the frosty bushes. There were a lot of tears. Many of the birds had been taken down from their perches and were now sitting on shoulders, woven into hair-dos, lying as if drunk or dead on the floor. A robin lay face-down in the cheese wheel we had instead of a cake.

My final memory of the wedding is of my best man, Hugo, standing in the driveway with twinkling lights behind him, waving. On his shoulder was a robin that seemed to be waving too, wishing us luck and love on the road ahead. Which, by and large, we've had.

My favourite book about the robin, that jaunty, bloodthirsty bird, is *Redbreast* by Andrew Lack, published in 2008 as a re-working of a book by his father, the eminent ornithologist David, which came out in 1950.[1] In *Redbreast*, the robin appears in his many literary guises, from the kindly sprite who comes to cover the bodies of the babes in the wood in folklore, to the traditional friend of prisoners, to the jolly little bird of Christmas cards and spade handles.[2] Lack is upfront about the flaw at the heart of the project. Early on he says: 'There are no truly great robin poems . . . the robin simply isn't that kind of heroic, elusive creature. Its literature has a clarity and directness that echo those of the bird itself . . . Robins are unambiguous, democratic, up-front.'

We moved to the country in mid-winter, with snow falling but not settling and mud everywhere. The old rectory we'd bought was unfinished and draught-haunted, plonked in a mire of thick Kentish clay. It was a bleak time, with friends suddenly far away, and no theatre, or friendly local bookshop, or sushi. There was a robin, though, living in the shed in the garden. My son named him Mr Bulldozer and set about taming him, and his full-hearted song, what Emily Brontë called his 'wildly tender' music, gave comfort as we waited out that winter of brutal storms and encroaching mud.

Another light came from a book. My plumber, Kevin, told me that the priest who'd lived in the rectory before us had been the nature correspondent for the *Wealden Times*; his parishioners had collected together his columns in a book when he retired. I tracked it down and have a copy on my desk – *From a Country Rectory Window* by John Green, on its cover a picture of what is now my study window, rose-grown and rusticated. Birds flit through the pages of Green's book, with the priest coming across as a decent, old-fashioned man, his prose careful and unadorned.[3] He writes of the nightingales he hears in his orchard (they've moved over the road, but still thrill on late summer evenings). He writes of the ducks that nest in the pond, and of local boys who come to fish for eel (the pond has silted up, it'll be next year's job to dredge it). He writes of robins. He seems to have felt a particular fondness for the 'little home-sweet bird' who trilled outside the rectory, or came in through the church's clerestory windows to sing along with the carols. He tells of one bright Mothering Sunday when, 'As we sang the concluding hymn "For the Beauty of the Earth," a robin flew into the sanctuary, bringing the outside world more obviously into our vocal praise.'

In 'The Woodman', John Clare calls the robin 'tamest of the feathered race', and Emily Dickinson figures it as the most domestic of birds.[4]

> The robin is the one
> That speechless from her nest
> Submits that home and certainty
> And sanctity are best.

William Hazlitt said that he'd rather have a robin beside him than a friend or a lover: 'give me the robin redbreast, pecking the crumbs at the door, or warbling on the leafless spray, the same glancing form that has followed me wherever I have been and "done its spiriting gently".' I like to imagine that the robin would, in turn, approve of his companion Hazlitt — radical, solitary, proud, possessed of a style that's scintillating in its clarity and elegance.

Edward Grey tamed robins at the end of his life — I've already mentioned the photograph of him, ancient, smiling, with a robin perched on his cap. He did this 'not with any intention of scientific observation, but solely for the pleasure of being on terms of intimacy with birds in a free and natural state.' In *The Charm of Birds*, he tames a robin he calls White Feather, who 'would sit on my fingers and eat meal-worms out of a little box held open on the hand.' He gives detailed instructions on how to establish relations with the birds, and we picture the aged statesman in stiff tweed prostrate before the robin, his friend. 'Any male robin can be tamed,' he writes:

> such at least is my experience. The bird is first attracted by crumbs of bread thrown on the ground; then a meal-worm is thrown to it; then a box – such as one of the small metal boxes in which chemists sell lozenges – is placed open on the ground with meal-worms in it. When the bird has become used to this, the next step is to kneel down and place the back of one hand flat upon the ground with the box open in the upturned palm, and the fingers projecting beyond the box. This is the most difficult stage, but robins will risk their lives for meal-worms, and the bird will soon face the fingers and stand on them. The final stage, that of getting the bird to come onto the hand when raised above the ground, is easy. The whole process may be a matter of only two or three days in hard weather, when birds are hungry, and once it has been accomplished the robin does not lose its tameness: confidence has been established and does not diminish when weather becomes mild and food plentiful.

It is in winter, though, that we need the robin most, because he's often the only one singing (and is one of the few instances where the thoughtless masculine pronoun is incorrect: the winter song comes from both males and females, with the male only taking over exclusive singing rights in spring). If you're standing in a high, cold wind and a clear, brave babble of notes falls down around you, you can be sure it's a robin. John Clare conveys something of the chilly comfort the bird offers:

> Sweet little bird in russet coat,
> The livery of the closing year,
> I love thy lonely plaintive note
> And tiny whispering song to hear,
> While on the stile or garden seat

I sit to watch the falling leaves,
The song thy little joys repeat
My loneliness relieves.

In 'A Dream of Winter', W.H. Davies writes of hearing the robin in autumn and finding winter in the icy notes of the bird's song:

It is the Robin, singing of
A silver world of snow and frost;
Where all is cold and white—except
The fire that's on his own warm breast.

Robins still sing in spring, but often their voices are lost in the throaty tumult of blackbirds, warblers, woodpeckers – all the busy breeding chatter. We hear them in autumn and winter because they are out there on their own, letting out what Edward Thomas calls 'sad songs of autumn mirth'. When William Sharp[5] hears a robin singing in the Grove of Academe, where Plato taught, he's at once transported to:

a lonely isle
Far in the Hebrides
An isle where all day long
The redbreast's song
Goes fluting on the wind o'er lonely sands.

The sadness of the robin's song is picked up in Elizabeth Gaskell's *North and South*, where Margaret, the heroine, is walking dejectedly in the garden. She's just heard the news that she and her family must leave the rectory at Helstone – 'Helstone is like a village in a poem—in one of Tennyson's poems,' she says – and go north. Her father, a dissenter, has had a crisis of faith and has given up his position, a move that overthrows all of Margaret's dreams, snatching away the prospect of following her sister into a happy marriage. The robin is the soundtrack to this moment of autumnal melancholy, her father's solicitude to the bird presented in stark contrast to the homelessness he has forced on his family.

> Margaret moved stiffly and slowly away from the place in the hall where she had been standing so long, out through the bare echoing drawing-room, into the twilight of an early November evening. There was a filmy veil of soft dull mist obscuring, but not hiding, all objects, giving them a lilac hue, for the sun had not yet fully set; a robin was singing – perhaps, Margaret thought, the very robin that her father had so often talked of as his winter pet, and for which he had made, with his own hands, a kind of robin-house by his study-window. The leaves were more gorgeous than ever; the first touch of frost would lay them all low on the ground. Already one or two kept constantly floating down, amber and golden in the low slanting sun-rays . . . Even now, while she walked sadly through that damp and drear garden in the dusk, with everything falling and fading, and turning to decay around her . . . Here there was no sound. The robin had gone away into the vast stillness of night.

The quintessential literary robin, though, is that of Frances Hodgson Burnett in *The Secret Garden*. I have a copy of the book in a hessian cover embroidered by my great-great-grandmother, Joanna, a farmer's wife from northern Indiana, who clipped it from *The American Magazine* when it was first published in instalments in 1910.[6] I pass the house which inspired the novel, Great Maytham Hall, on my way to the Waterstones in Tenterden, and drop in the three or four times a year it opens its doors to the public. I feel an enormous fondness for Hodgson Burnett's old-fashioned story and its chipper robin, whose company helps Mary shrug off her un-Victorian slovenliness (and her unfortunate nick-name). 'Mistress Mary forgot that she had ever been contrary in her life when he allowed her to draw closer and closer to him, and bend down and talk and try to make something like robin sounds.'

I like to think that it's some contemporary offspring of Mary's robin that hops through the pages of Scarlett Thomas's luminous and visionary *The Seed Collectors*. There's an extraordinary passage in which the robin, who has been feeding on magical seeds, takes on a voice like a vorticist poem:

> The man is, as always, incompt and untrig. He sloggers around his rooms in his black and grey ragtails like an elderly magpie with those bleep bleep noises going all around him, a choir of dying things. The bleep bleep noises sometimes enter the robins licham and make him abubble and a little gunpowdered . . .
>
> Man gives the robin a halfpod. After the pod the robin's flight is swipping and meteorous and he does not need to visit the bird table at all. He is wick! He is fire-swift! He can also sit in stilth and ro for longtimes and mull, and for a time he forgets about the sparrowhawks and pussycats and the long grey squirrel. In his merrow head he hears whirleries of human poetry and other meaningthings fro far, far away . . . After eating the podseeds the robin singsandsings, and thinksgreatthoughts and balladsmuch long after darkness comes.

On the other side of the image of robin as the home-bird, the sprightly greeter of postmen, the Christmas spade-percher, is a vicious and territory-mad villain, a thug and a bully. Philip Hoare wrote in *the Guardian* of his dislike of the robin, which had just been chosen as Britain's favourite bird in a poll:

> Highly aggressive and territorial, that sweet song fluting from your fence is actually the avian equivalent of a foul-mouthed 'get orf my land.' Males will peck at rivals' napes to sever their spinal cords – 10% of all adult robin deaths are robin-on-robin, red-on-red incidents. They also launch unprovoked attacks on other, innocent species, lashing out with razor-sharp claws.

This shadow-side is reflected in the work I'd hold up as a riposte to Andrew Lack's claim that the robin can't inspire great poetry. Robert Graves's 'The

Christmas Robin' is chilling, full of foreboding. I found it in an old paperback of his 'Selected Poems', copying it into my notebook in the February of my first year of university, when ice formed on the inside of my study windows. Written in that dark decade, the 1930s, it looks ahead to a world of 'more snow, and worse than snow'. The robin's song will never sound blithe or innocent again, and suddenly the robins that illuminated the winter forest of my wedding speak of a future more ambiguous and uncertain.

> The snows of February had buried Christmas
> Deep in the woods, where grew self-seeded
> The fir-trees of a Christmas yet unknown,
> Without a candle or a strand of tinsel.
>
> Nevertheless when, hand in hand, plodding
> Between the frozen ruts, we lovers paused
> And 'Christmas trees!' cried suddenly together,
> Christmas was there again, as in December.
>
> We velveted our love with fantasy
> Down a long vista-row of Christmas trees,
> Whose coloured candles slowly guttered down
> As grandchildren came trooping round our knees.
>
> But he knew better, did the Christmas robin –
> The murderous robin with his breast aglow
> And legs apart, in a spade-handle perched:
> He prophesied more snow, and worse than snow.

GREY HERON

My CHILDREN GREW UP with the 'long-necked heron, dread of nimble eels'.[1] We moved across London when my son was two, my daughter about to make an appearance after a nervy pregnancy. For six months before the move my wife had been confined to her bed and so, whenever I could, I'd take my son out of the house – first in a backpack, then on his own sturdy little legs. We'd join the Grand Union Canal at Haggerston and walk up to the green-fringed darkness of the Islington tunnel, then back past drab estates and cool white houses, and always we'd see a grey heron, eerily still in winter light.[2]

If we'd thought about it, we could have done away with the pantechnicon and loaded our things onto a barge to move home. We ended up in Kensal Green, overlooking the cemetery, where the graves led down towards the banks of the same canal, six miles to the west. The cemetery was dense with birds – gaudy rose-ringed parakeets, choiring blackbirds and song-thrushes, bouncing green woodpeckers. Still the greatest joy for me and for my kids (my daughter strapped into the back seat of my bike, my son wobbling dangerously near to the water on his) were the herons. There were more here in NW10, equally still in the shadows of abandoned warehouses and haulage depots. They made us still, too, leaning on our bicycles until the swift jab of the yellow dagger bill into the water. Or, even better, when they struggled with grace into the London sky and we stood below, dumbstruck, waving our own arms and laughing.

In flight the heron is atavistic, stately even – 'outlandish' is John Clare's word for him. Robert MacFarlane calls them pterodactyls, and he's right – no other bird makes sixty-five million years seems so short. Mary Oliver sees them 'rowing forward into flight'[3] and in 'Audubon: A Vision', Robert Penn Warren used the same image:

> the large bird,
> Long neck outthrust, wings crooked to scull air, moved
> In a slow calligraphy, crank, flat and black against
> The colour of God's blood spilt, as though
> Pulled by a string.

From the new house, we'd walk up the canal to the heronry in Regent's Park to see the fledglings in their nests: twenty adult birds, a 'heron priested shore'[4] on a pond less than a mile from Oxford Circus. Occasionally there'd be RSPB volunteers there who'd let us – me holding my daughter, my son on tip-toes – look at the birds up-close through telescopes. The herons stood as still in the trees as they did in the water, before rising massively into the air at the clacking command of their scrawny chicks. The nests were huge, perilous – John Clare says they 'load the trees till nearly broken down'.

It was one of these Regent's Park birds I thought of when I came across a Virginia Woolf story, 'Monday or Tuesday', which is told from the viewpoint of a heron: 'Lazy and indifferent,' it begins, 'shaking space easily from his wings, knowing his way, the heron passes over the church beneath the sky.' It's less a story, more a six-paragraph prose-poem, the heron sweeping over the roofs of a city, dipping down into snippets of conversation, the pealing of a lunchtime bell, the clamour of tradespeople and omnibuses. The final paragraphs spiral out into luxurious visions of a world of 'the marble square pendant, minarets beneath and the Indian seas, while space rushes blue and stars glint'. Finally, as dusk falls, the heron returns to his roost, as if unmoved by the vibrant, multifarious spectacle that passed beneath him: 'Lazy and indifferent the heron returns; the sky veils her stars; then bares them.'

When Michael Longley's great friend, the American writer Kenneth Koch, died of leukaemia in 2002, Longley wrote an elegy, 'The Heron', that performed a kind of metamorphosis of remembrance. Koch died as Longley was driving down to his cottage at Carrigskeewaun in County Mayo, and over the course of the poem, the gangly Koch becomes the heron, flying upwards until it attains a synoptic view of the world, shrinking the distance between Longley and his dying friend. The refrain in the poem – 'I didn't know' – beats with the same slow flap as the bird's wings and the rhythm, lifting towards the end, seems to echo the lumbering take-off of this great, sad bird.

> You are so tall and skinny I shall conscript a heron
> To watch over you on hang-glider wings, old soldier.
> . . .
> Tuck your head in like a heron and trail behind you
> Your long legs, take to the air above a townland
> That encloses Carrigskeewaun and Central Park.

There's a passage that's equally lyrical and elegiac in Thomas Hardy's *The Return of the Native*. The weary, despairing Mrs Yeobright is trudging across Egdon Heath and catches sight of a heron in flight. There's something angelic about the heron, caught in the rays of the evening sun, but also a coldness – it's as if the bird himself plays a part in 'pinioning' Mrs Yeobright to the earth, perhaps he's even an envoy of the ruthless natural world that'll kill her, a few pages later, with the bite of an adder.

> While she looked a heron arose on that side of the sky and flew on with his face towards the sun. He had come dripping wet from some pool in the valleys, and as he flew the edges and lining of his wings, his thighs and his breast were so caught by the bright sunbeams that he appeared as if formed of burnished silver. Up in the zenith where he was seemed

a free and happy place, away from all contact with the earthly ball to which she was pinioned; and she wished that she could arise uncrushed from its surface and fly as he flew then.

There is something unsettling about these great, still birds. We sense in them a deep sorrow as they stand for hours, caught in brown studies over grey water. In 'Gray Herons in the Field above the River', W.S. Merwin sees them as:

shadows of ourselves risen out of our shadows
each eye without turning continues to behold
what is moving.

In a short story by W. B. Yeats called 'The Old Men of the Twilight', St Patrick curses the 'men of learning' who will not cease their whittling to hear the news he brings. In a 'strange voice in which there was a rapture as of one speaking from behind a battlement of Druid flame,' the saint says:

I shall make you an example for ever and ever; you shall become grey herons and stand pondering in grey pools and flit over the world in that hour when it is most full of sighs; and you shall preach to the other herons until they are also like you; and your deaths shall come by chance and unforeseen, for you shall not be certain about anything for ever and ever.

John Clare picked up on the wretchedness of the heron in one of his greatest poems, 'High Overhead that Silent Throne'. He calls the bird a 'crane' here, but in *Birdscapes* Jeremy Mynott argues conclusively that Clare is referring to the grey heron, which bore the local name of heronshaw or crane in Clare's fenland home.[5] We are still thrilled whenever we see herons passing overhead, but once you read Clare's mournful lines, it's hard to avoid sensing a kind of dejectedness in the bird's slow flight, the suggestion of a creature just about ready to throw it all in.[6]

High overhead that silent throne
Of wild and cloud betravelled sky
That makes ones loneliness more lone
Sends forth a crank and reedy cry
I look the crane is sailing oer
That pathless world without a mate
The heath looked brown and dull before
But now tis more then desolate

With the heron, though, we return to that stillness, the sense of a bird whose capacity for waiting will outlast our own. Vernon Watkins says that 'no distraction breaks the watch / Of that time-killing bird'[7] and yet we always feel that those canny yellow eyes are as much on us as they are on the fish below. The heron waits in a world of perpetual potential, for contained within that vigilant pose are his three possibilities:

flight:

'it struggles
into its wings then soars sunwards and throws
its huge overcoat across the earth;'[8]

food:

'the heron blinds the white river cornea with the spear of his bill;'[9]

or merely to continue waiting:

'Motionless under the moon-beam,
Up to his feathers in the stream.'[10]

CROW

I N THE LIVING ROOM of Ennet House, the drying-out clinic in David Foster Wallace's *Infinite Jest*, two of the residents are talking about sadness. It's 2.45 a.m. and Geoffrey Day, privileged, urbane, a 'red-wine-and-Quaalude man who ... manned the helm of a Scholarly Journal' is telling Kate Gompert, sufferer of 'dead-eyed anhedonia', about the onset of his depression. As a boy, he says, he was playing the violin and the notes, mingled with the hum of a fan, set off a dreadful resonance. 'It was as if a large dark billowing shape came ... flapping out of some backwater of my psyche.' The shape in Day's mind summoned feelings of 'total horror. It was all horror everywhere, distilled and given form ... It rose and grew larger and became engulfing and more horrible than I shall ever have the power to convey.'

Slowly, Day reaches to describe the shape, which was 'dark, and either billowing or flapping'. He tells Kate that it was like 'a small part of the wing of something far too large to be seen in totality. It was total psychic horror: death, decay, dissolution, cold empty black malevolent lonely voided space. It was the worst thing I have ever confronted.' There is a moment of connection between the two as Gompert condenses the conversation into one ghastly, lyrical image: 'Time in the shadow of the wing of the thing too big to see, rising.'[1]

When they were small, my kids loved Aldous Huxley's *The Crows of Pearblossom*. Huxley wrote the story on Christmas Eve, 1944, for his niece, Olivia de Hauleville, who'd come to spend extended periods at Huxley's house in the Mojave desert. The crows in it are American everymen: the wife a put-upon homemaker, the husband a harried pharmacist. I wonder – painfully – how long it will be before these benign, genial crows are replaced in their young imaginations with the dark, lumbering beasts that I know, crows like a bruise on the mind, boding nothing good. In his *The Parliament of Fowls*, Chaucer writes of the 'ill-omened crow', and the corvidae family, particularly the black tricksters, the gothic perchers – the carrion crow and its bulky inflation, the raven – are the signature birds of despair.[2]

Insomnia afflicts people in different ways; mine wakes me in the greyness before sunrise. I've written elsewhere about the joy of a dawn chorus, but sometimes it's the loneliest time, particularly if there's no song but the long broken creak of the crow. When we lived in Kensal Green, I used to wake roiled in the blackest thoughts at some hour too early to rise but too late to get back to sleep. There was no birdsong in those tight-pressed sooty streets, but the crows that stepped up and down our roof, hawking and croaking, seemed to give voice to my howling fantods, a soundtrack to those hours of worry and regret. They seemed – and this doesn't feel like an exaggeration – evil.[3]

The painting that was on Van Gogh's easel when he killed himself was *Wheatfield with Crows*, and showed an unpeopled landscape, black birds rising threateningly over it, a road winding into the empty distance, dark clouds massing. It is thought that it was in this very field, with the crows circling over, that Van Gogh 'erased his own map', as Wallace might have it, firing a revolver into his chest before walking back to a hotel in Auvers-sur-Oise to die, two days later, with some cheerful last words: *'la tristesse durera toujours'*. It perhaps explains why the painting is able to summon such melancholy out of an unexceptional rural scene. It is a vision, as Van Gogh wrote in a letter to his younger brother a month before his death, *'de la solitude extrême'*.

Crows are birds of graveyards, of still-smoking battlefields, of plague pits and charnel-houses, but they also haunt the ruined landscapes of the mind. Early last year, as I read Max Porter's *Grief is the Thing With Feathers*, in which an academic writing about Ted Hughes's *Crow* is visited by the bird, I remember thinking of the billowing wing in *Infinite Jest*. Porter's protagonist is the happily married father of two small boys whose life is shattered when his wife falls, hits her head and dies. His crow is, initially, like Day's wing, an objective correlative of his despair. He feels 'Feathers between my fingers, in my eyes, in my mouth, beneath me a feathery hammock lifting me up a foot above the tiled floor . . . Put. Me. Down, I croaked, and my piss warmed the cradle of his wing.'

In 'How Many Nights', a beautiful short poem by Galway Kinnell, he describes lying awake, seized by unnamed terrors, of fears that evaporate with the morning sun, when he walks out 'over the frozen world' with all its hidden winter life. And yet there is a reminder of the night's darkness that will not be banished by nature's soft whispering voices.

> above me
> a wild crow crying *'yaw yaw yaw'*
> from a branch nothing cried from ever in my life.

The crow carries traces of the night in his dark feathers and seems, like the robin, a bird of the winter, maybe only because he is loud and present when so much else is absent. In 'February', Boris Pasternak sets rooks and crows against a bleak backdrop. 'February. Get out the ink and weep!' the poem begins, and goes on to send rooks falling through the sky like 'charred pears'. It is a ruthlessly colourless poem, with the white of the landscape and the black of the crows building to a forlorn final stanza — the birds on the snow metamorphose into letters on a page:

> There gaps open black in the snow's expanse
> And the crow-pocked wind throbs
> And the surest poems come by chance
> Wrought from sobs.[4]

Thomas Lovell Beddoes finally managed to kill himself in February 1849 in Basel, Switzerland. He was forty-five. His first attempt, in October of the previous year, when he'd tried to sever an artery in his leg, had left him gangrenous and wheelchair-bound. After surgery to amputate the leg, he got hold of curare, an Amazonian arrow poison, and addressed his suicide note to a friend in England. 'I ought to have been among other things a good poet,' he wrote, but instead was now 'food for what I am good for—worms.' He enjoined his friend to make his own mind up as to whether any of Beddoes's remaining work should be published.

Beddoes was the foremost exponent of the now-forgotten Elizabethan/Jacobean revival that took place in the mid-nineteenth century, and was alcoholic and death-obsessed. He wrote a series of poems in the mode of Donne and Marvell, the best of which, 'Dream Pedlary', John Ashbery called 'one of the most seamlessly beautiful lyrics in the English language'.[5] In it, Beddoes addresses his 'lov'd long-lost boy' and dwells on death and the spirits that swirl around him. Beddoes was allowed to watch his father, a famous surgeon, perform dissections while he was a child and had, as the critic H.W. Donner put it, a 'skeleton complex'.

As Beddoes moved from promising youth – he was at Pembroke, Oxford, a few years after Shelley and was spoken of as a potential successor – to dissolute early middle age, he became more and more taken up with a long verse play called *Death's Jest Book*. It was only finally published after his suicide in 1850, but a first draft appears to have been finished as early as 1830. He spent the final years of his life – when he wasn't setting fire to the Drury Lane playhouse with a lighted five pound note in protest at the mediocrity of the play he'd just seen, or renting out a theatre in Frankfurt so that his lover, a baker named Konrad Degen, might act out scenes from Shakespeare – writing and re-writing his own play. It was, as Ashbery says, 'a kind of bottomless pit that absorbed most of his creative energies during his final years.'

Death's Jest Book is a revenge tragedy set in thirteenth-century Germany, although there are frequent, rather disconcerting journeys to Egypt. Beddoes himself took a kind of glee in how difficult it was, writing to a friend: 'I think it will be entertaining, very unamiable, & utterly unpopular.' The play/poem is partly a pastiche, partly a genuinely unsettling attempt to reveal to the reader the horror and absurdity of death. It is full of shape-shifting characters, murder, witchcraft and some lines of extraordinary lyricism. 'Wolfram's Song', which comes just after the malevolent antagonist Isbrand has seized power in Grüssau, introduces us to Beddoes' beloved chthonic crow. It's a ghost shanty: gory and ghoulish and wonderful:

> Old Adam, the carrion crow,
> The old crow of Cairo;
> He sat in the shower, and let it flow
> Under his tail and over his crest;
> And through every feather
> Leak'd the wet weather;
> And the bough swung under his nest;
> For his beak it was heavy with marrow.
> Is that the wind dying? O no;
> It's only two devils, that blow,
> Through a murderer's bones, to and fro,
> In the ghosts' moonshine.

While many have compared Beddoes's play to the absurdism of Beckett or Brecht, the critic Ian Bamforth suggests another association. 'Beddoes's Old Adam—the "carrion crow"—seems to anticipate Ted Hughes's baleful anthropomorphic[6] creature of the same name.'[7] There's something almost unseemly about the closeness forged between the crow and the poet in Hughes's sequence.[8] The *Crow* poems are rarely lovely as poetry – Hughes himself described the poems as 'songs with no music whatsoever, in a super simple and super-ugly language' – but they contain, for me at least, something just as important: they crackle with instress, they allow the bird to own his myth. Hughes's crow – tricky, bawdy, nihilistic, uproarious – dances across the page, trawling with him a rancid rag-and-bone shop of dashed hopes and dark visions.

Hughes's crow takes wing against a complex mythological backdrop, from creation to the final fall. Hauntingly ritualistic passages are interwoven with evocations of the bird in nature, creating an animal character that doesn't seem like a theft from the human world, but exists on its own terms. Crow is 'a black rainbow / Bent in emptiness / over emptiness / But flying.' He is 'Screaming for Blood / Grubs, crusts / Anything.' He is brutal and yet vulnerable, as when 'He found a dead mole and slowly he took it apart / Then stared at the gobbets, feeling helpless.' Crow is 'spraddled head-down in the beach-garbage, guzzling a dropped ice-cream.' At the end of the book, looking out on a ruined world, the crow sits in a palace of skulls:

> His crown is the last splinters
> Of the vessel of life.
> His throne is the scaffold of bones, the hanged thing's
> Rack and final stretcher.

The epic folk-tale of Hughes's *Crow* provides a lens through which to view the events of the blood-soaked twentieth century. It's hard to read it without picturing the camps and the gulags, the death-marches and atom bombs. And yet always there, despite ourselves, we can't help but see a traumatised Hughes writing the poems after the suicide of one wife, in the lead-up to the suicide and infanticide of another, finding in his crow a rowdy, male, inhuman companion to cackle and croak him through the darkest hours. The political and domestic worlds, both fallen into ruin.

Max Porter's *Grief is a Thing with Feathers* picks up on the image of the crow as a nursemaid to sorrow. The bird helps the broken narrator navigate his loss by allowing him access to lacerating rage, to deep, animal grief. This is a very different crow to Hughes's, though, despite the bird telling the narrator to 'please remember I am your Ted's song-legend, Crow of the death-chill, please. The God-eating, trash-licking, word-murdering, carcass-desecrating mathbomb motherfucker, and all that.' Indeed, one of the great delights of the book is seeing how Porter plays with our familiarity with Hughes's *Crow*, undercutting our expectations of the bird at every point, entering into a richly fertile dialogue with the earlier book.

It is as if Porter is asking us to understand that in the almost half-century that lies between Hughes's *Crow* and his own *Grief* ... our conception of the world, of domestic life, of masculinity, have all changed utterly. Porter's crow is 'a babysitting bird ... an authorised and accredited caregiver, much admired by London parents, much in demand of a Friday night.' He is soft and sensitive behind his bluster, funny and almost feminine in places. He repeatedly assures the narrator 'I won't leave until you don't need me any more.' He is, one feels, a rebuke to Hughes's *Crow*, to Hughes's world-view, but a gentle, sentimental one.

There's one final crow I'd like to bring out, one who acts upon the reader much as Hughes's crow, as Porter's act: reminding us of chaos, of darkness, of the black animal world outside our windows. The crow in D.H. Lawrence's 'In Church' carries echoes of old myths to the rite of Christian sacrament, a literal blot on the tranquility of the scene. It's necessary, though, this 'soft full drop of darkness' for without it says Lawrence, Hughes, Porter, say I, there would be no light, and we'd go the way of Van Gogh and DFW, disappearing under the shadow of the crow's wing.

> In the choir the boys are singing the hymn.
> 　　The morning light on their lips
> Moves in silver-moist flashes, in musical trim.
>
> Sudden outside the high window, one crow
> 　　Hangs in the air
> And lights on a withered oak-tree's top of woe.
>
> One bird, one blot, folded and still at the top
> 　　Of the withered tree!—in the grail
> Of crystal heaven falls one full black drop.
>
> Like a soft full drop of darkness it seems to sway
> 　　In the tender wine
> Of our Sabbath, suffusing our sacred day.

CURLEW

T WO OF THE THREE or four Western avian extinctions since the Great
Auk in 1852 were curlews. Fred Bosworth's 1955 novel, *Last of the Curlews*,
is written from the perspective of the final remaining eskimo curlew on earth
as he undertakes his migration from the Canadian Arctic to the Pampas of
Patagonia. Bosworth does his best not to anthropomorphise the bird, but the
passages in which the curlew briefly meets and then loses his mate, as they fly over
the Andes and up across the plains of the Midwest, are a kind of tragic road-trip,
the birds' fragile, wind-buffeted union beautiful and doomed.

Equally powerful is Horatio Clare's *Orison for a Curlew*, which sees the
author set off on a hopeless quest in search of the slender-billed curlew.[1] This
slim book, written in lapidary prose, chases the ghost of the vanished bird 'of
delicate appearance and mysterious habits' through Greece and the Balkans,
with Clare speaking to ornithologists and environmentalists whose valiant
actions were too little, too late.

It seems fitting, somehow, that the melancholy curlew, whose eldritch cry
has stirred fear and sown sorrow over the centuries, should be amongst the
avant garde of the great Holocene extinction event, its sad call an unheeded
warning of the wave of extinctions to come.

In the Old English poem 'The Seafarer', written deep in the Dark Ages, the anonymous author looks back on his life amid waves and sea-birds, driving the 'foam-furrow' far from home. The poet is an outsider, frozen and friendless, exiled to roam the icy and unforgiving oceans. The curlew is the spirit bird of the poem, its long sorrowful call lilting down through the wretched lines:[2]

Hwilum ylfete song	At times the swan's song
dyde ic me to gomene,	I took to myself as pleasure,
ganotes hleoþor	the gannet's noise
ond huilpan sweg	and the voice of the curlew
fore hleahtor wera,	instead of the laughter of men,
mæw singende	the singing gull
fore medodrince.	instead of the drinking of mead.

The curlew is a bird of desolate places, of moors and bleak estuaries, of winter dusk and dreich weather. W.H. Hudson describes the call, which is a rising and desperate one, as 'uttered by some filmy being, half spirit and half bird.' Dylan Thomas addresses a herd 'Ho, hullabulloing clan / Agape, with woe / In your beaks.'

Memories seem to cleave to the curlew's call, so I cannot hear it without a rush of unhappy recollections, dark visions and regrets. It's a bird best appreciated alone and sad-hearted. In one of Yeats's most beautiful lyrics, 'He Reproves the Curlew', the mythical figure of Red Hanrahan finds the bird's song tilts him into despair for a lost love:

O CURLEW, cry no more in the air,
Or only to the water in the West;
Because your crying brings to my mind
passion-dimmed eyes and long heavy hair
That was shaken out over my breast:
There is enough evil in the crying of wind.

Ted Hughes borrows that call to echo the melancholy moorland of 'Horses', where 'I listened in emptiness on the moor-ridge. / The curlew's tear turned its edge on the silence.' For Tennyson it is the sound of the gothic grandeur of Locksley Hall: ''T is the place, and all around it, as of old, the curlews call, / Dreary gleams about the moorland flying over Locksley Hall.' There's no bird that seems so firmly fitted to this atmosphere of desolation: it is a creature of dim light, of dank and dismal air. As Richard Mabey puts it, 'birdsongs seem to have been scored to fit their surroundings. The lilting of curlews on an empty moor . . . '[3] In 'Curlew', the Scottish poet Norman MacCaig hears the birds' song and it conjures a landscape:

> trailing bubbles of music . . .
> Music as desolate, as beautiful
> as your loved places.
> mountainy marshes and glistening mudflats
> by the stealthy sea.

In folklore, both in Britain and abroad, the ominous Seven Whistlers are curlews. It is said that the night-time call of the birds – lost souls searching for home – foretells a death.[4] In Spenser's *The Fairie Queene*, Sir Guyon and his squire, Palmer, have just arrived on the island of Acrasia when a thick mist descends. In the air around them, winged creatures flap and shriek, each portending ill:

> all the nation of unfortunate
> And fatall birds about them flocked were,
> Such as by nature men abhorre and hate,
> The ill-faste Owle, deaths dreadfull messengere,
> The hoars Night-raven, trump of dolefull drere,
> The lether-winged Bat, dayes enimy,
> The ruefull Strich, still waiting on the bere,
> The Whistler shrill, that who so heares, doth dy,
> The hellish Harpies, prophets of sad destiny.

My copy of the poem, which I studied at university and remember struggling with, not unpleasantly, parses the Strich as a little owl and the Whistler as a curlew.

Curlews often fly and call at night, and the sound of a flock passing overhead, dropping down their uncanny cries through the darkness, is truly creepy. In 'The Curlew Cried,'[5] written some four centuries after *The Fairie Queene* and on the other side of the world, the Australian poet and Aboriginal rights campaigner Oodgeroo Noonuccal spoke of the curlew's cry coming 'out of the Shadow Land'. It was the 'loneliest voice that earth knows'. As in British folklore, the bird's call carries sinister connotations:

> Three nights they heard the curlew cry.
> It is the warning known of old
> That tells them one tonight shall die.

Wherever curlews call – and their range is vast, both the Eurasian curlew heard from Siberia to Japan, from Britain to North Africa, and its American and Antipodean kin – they are associated with this eerie, hopeless mourning.

In 'Loch Thom' by W.S. Graham, the poet revisits a well-loved childhood spot, where he hears:

> The same
> Long-beaked cry curls across
> The heather-edges of the water.

He finds that, despite the years that have passed since he last visited the place, 'The curlew's cry travelling still / Kills me fairly'. He leaves in a kind of panic, haunted by the past and stalked by the call. Similarly, for Idris Davies in 'The Curlews of Blaen Rhymni', the voice of the birds is at once beautiful and terrible as he walks through the Welsh hills at night. 'And the crying of the curlew makes more sad and strange and fair / The moon above the moorland and the clear midnight air.' The poet recognises, like Bai Juyi in 'Hearing the

Early Oriole', that we change as we age and birdsong changes with us, so that we may not step twice into the same stream of song.

> And curlew calls to curlew, and I remember as I go
> The merrier sounds and echoes out of seasons long ago,
> When the nights were full of laughter and all the days were bright
> And the heart too young to listen to the curlew in the night.

Melancholy is not all the curlew offers, though, as the children in Molly Keane's *Full House* recognise. Nick, a neighbour of the Bird family (the indomitable matriarch of the house is Lady Bird), lives by himself in 'a painfully white cottage on the extreme point of a low and rocky peninsula'. He's a 'queer man' with his:

> light wild eyes as quick as a bird's He never looked quite human or like other people. He was too much alone. There was a kind of curlew sadness about him, or perhaps more the sadness of a woodcock, for there was nothing faëry about Nick, as there is about a curlew.

Now I love woodcocks, but I do see that there's something elevated about the curlew, that it is ethereal, elemental in a way that the woodcock is not, its long literary and folkloric history delivering it from the merely gloomy to an image at once austere, poetic, otherworldly and solitary.

It's this element of nobility that Seamus Heaney drew upon in 'From the Republic of Conscience', written in 1986 to commemorate the twenty-fifth anniversary of the founding of Amnesty International. Unusually for Heaney, it's a kind of fable, where conscience is an island, a place where people are able to live in dignified self-sufficiency. Describing the composition of the poem, he said:

> Conscience is a republic, a silent, solitary place where a person would find it hard to avoid self-awareness and self-examination; and this made

me think of Orkney. I remembered the silence the first time I landed there. When I got off the small propeller plane and started walking across the grass to a little arrivals hut, I heard the cry of a curlew.[6]

It's a more upbeat interpretation of the bird's song – lonely, but courageous with it. Heaney begins:

> When I landed in the republic of conscience
> it was so noiseless when the engines stopped
> I could hear a curlew high above the runway.

You need that silence, Heaney seems to say, in order to be *with yourself*. If you can hear the call of a curlew, you'll hear the other deep and necessary voices – of decency, of authenticity, of conscience.

It's hard to believe, when you see a vast herd of curlew bobbing those decurving bills over a flooded winter field or massing on the vermiculated sands of an estuary, but these are birds in vertiginous decline. They're our largest wader and their size gives the impression of durability. Horatio Clare says 'they look warm even when they are up to their thighs in cold water, as they often are' – but numbers have fallen by over 50 per cent in the past quarter century and they've recently been added to the RSPB's red list.[7]

But before we fix too firmly on a purely dismal picture of the bird, it's worth remembering that there's a geographic bias to our encounters with curlews. Growing up in the South-East of England, my curlews were generally seen and heard in winter on the damp meadows of Pett Level near Rye or under the soused estuarine air of Pagham Harbour. For those in the North and West, the curlew's cry marks the coming of spring, as birds return to breed.

William Atkins, another South-Easterner, walking on Ted Hughes's Midgley Moor above the Calder Valley, notes how different the bird's call sounds in springtime:

> I heard the curlew, returned to the moor for the summer: a 'wobbling
> water call' was how Ted Hughes described it. I had heard winter flocks

of them on beaches, and yet that same sound, a drawling rippling trill, possessed a completely different quality when set against this solitude. It was magnificent in its strangeness. It was a sound I would grow to love.[8]

So we end on a joyful note, with the bird's voice an unearthly but welcome harbinger, not of death but of life, of spring. Edward Grey, far up in Fallodon, Northumberland, wrote:

> Of all bird songs or sounds known to me, there is none that I would prefer than the spring notes of the curlew . . . The notes do not sound passionate; they suggests peace, rest, healing joy, an assurance of happiness past, present and to come. To listen to curlews on a bright, clear April day, with the fullness of spring still in anticipation, is one of the best experiences that a lover of birds can have.

Similarly, Henry Williamson (whose politics could not be further from the genial liberalism of Grey), in Devon, writes of the curlew in *Tarka the Otter*:

> In early summer the wild spirit of the hills is heard in the voices of curlews. The birds fly up from solitary places, above their beloved and little ones, and float the wind in a sweet uprising music. Slowly on spread and hollow wings they sink, and their cries are trilling and cadent, until they touch earth and lift their wings above their heads, and poising, loose the last notes from their throats, like gold bubbles rising into the sky again.

WAXWING

MID-WAY ALONG THE JOURNEY of my life – I was thirty-three, rather than Dante's thirty-five – I began to drift. In spite of my two small children and a wife I loved, I took up a restless, peripatetic existence, wandering from one literary festival to the next, accepting journalistic commissions that flung me out to the world's forgotten edges. One late afternoon in November, 2012, I found myself crossing a bridge over railway tracks in Krasnoyarsk, Russia, close to the border with Mongolia. It's prison country there, and the railway station was the first destination for many of those released from the twenty-five high-security jails that surround the city. It was the end of a dreary afternoon and a raggedy group of men stood in the square outside the station hawking drugs and begging. Snow fell in damp flurries. It was minus 20°C.

I was at a literary festival in Siberia to speak about my novel, *This Bleeding City*, which had just been published in Russian. While I was there, though, I'd agreed to record a piece for BBC Radio 4 about a local monk. A one-time criminal and drug dealer, Andrey Peretz now ran a drying-out-centre-cum-spiritual-retreat, welcoming addicted prisoners straight off the train. I couldn't find his house, though. I wandered dejectedly up a rutted track between pines, jangling a handful of stones in one gloved hand and raising it occasionally if the stray dogs that barked and whimpered in the gloaming came too close.

I was about to give up and turn back towards the station when, outlined against the day's last light, I saw a rowan tree swaying and quivering as if alive. I moved closer and there, luminous even in the dimness, were two dozen waxwings, stripping the tree quickly and carefully of its bright red fruit.[1] The birds were just as Richard Dauenhauer, the poet laureate of Alaska, and an honorary member of the Tlingit tribe, described them in 'Gift of Bohemian Waxwings'. He gets the birds down so well he might as well have been there that day, on the other side of the Bering Strait, watching the masquerade of waxwings wrangle and throng.

> like fireworks against
> the lead November sky,
> harvesting the last of
> crimson berries, when
> the single bird explodes
> and all move on.

I was, for a moment, paralysed by their beauty. Then I crept carefully towards them until I was quite close to the tree and watched the jostling, jiving birds knock back berries like little shots of port. Their loveliness was so fierce, so out-of-place in that icy and wind-blasted world of prison camps and decaying factories that I wanted to fall to my knees. The waxwings, those exquisite birds with their lacquered quiffs, their berry-red and gorse-yellow cuffs and their woozy kohled eyes – they seemed to offer some kind of way out of the hole I'd dug myself into. Then, like Dauenhauer's exploding fireworks, they were off, and I watched them scatter across the sky over the railway yard.

As the last far dots of them disappeared, like flecks of confetti tossed to the evening wind, I found myself thinking of *Pale Fire*. This book had suffused my adolescence with its intense concoction of poetry, academia, Rider Haggard adventuring and birds.[2] The novel holds itself out as the final poem by the great (and entirely fictional) John Shade, heavily annotated by his colleague Charles Kinbote. As the tale unfurls, the reader learns that Kinbote is – or believes himself to be – the exiled King Charles Xavier of Nova Zembla, hiding from the ruthless Gradus, an assassin, in the leafy university town of New Wye. Shade's 999-line poem which forms the apparent heart of the book is partly valedictory, and in part an act of mourning for his daughter, who committed suicide after being stood up on a date. Her death is prefigured in the poem's opening lines.[3]

> I was the shadow of the waxwing slain[4]
> By the false azure in the window pane;
> I was the smudge of ashen fluff – and I
> Lived on, flew on, in the reflected sky

Kinbote's notes to the opening imagine Shade as a young man suffering his 'first eschatological shock' as a waxwing crashes against the glass and 'with incredulous fingers he picks up from the turf that compact ovoid body and gazes at the wax-red streaks ornamenting those gray-brown wings and at the graceful tail feathers tipped with yellow as bright as fresh paint.' In the index at the back of the book, Kinbote parses waxwings as 'birds of the genus *Bombycilla*' and notes a sub-species, *Bombycilla shadei*, named after John Shade's ornithologist father.

It seems to me that the waxwing, with its brigand's mask and unpredictable wanderings,[5] stands as a symbol of many of the book's central themes. *Pale Fire* is a novel about disguises and subterfuge, about meanings wrapped within meanings. It is a novel about a king from the frozen north forced abroad in search of safety, and about nostalgia and exile. It is, crucially, about fatherhood – it is no coincidence that Shade begins his poem with a waxwing, his father's bird, nor that, in the car-park of the Hawaiian bar where she has just been stood up, Hazel, Shade's daughter, sees iced puddles in which shimmer the 'azure entrance . . . neon-barred'. She, like the waxwing, has stared into the false reflection, and dies.

I wandered until darkness fell, up and down frozen rutted tracks, feeling lost in place and spirit. I met an old women who didn't speak English and gestured wildly at me before shrugging and trudging on into the thin snow. In German, the waxwing is known as the *Ungluckvogel* or *Todtenvogel*[6], perhaps on account of its sudden and unpredictable appearances. There's also, once you allow yourself to look at it that way, something sinister in the waxwing's mask and flushed cheeks, in the piratical get-up. I began to blame the waxwings for my predicament. In a poem by Stanley Plumly, 'Cedar Waxwing on Scarlet Firethorn', the birds arrive in the wake of a tragedy. It's my favourite poem in a wonderful American anthology of bird poetry called *Bright Wings*, edited by Billy Collins and given to me by my mother. 'To turn again to something beautiful, / And natural,' the poem begins. This is the story of another suicide: 'The good gun flowering in the mouth.' The waxwings move amongst the trees, persuading the poem's speaker that 'when we die what / lives is fluted on the air.'[7]

> the waxwing first on one
> foot, then the other, holding the berry
> against the moment like a drop of blood –
> red-wing-tipped, yellow at the tip of the
> tail, the head sleek, crested, fin or arrow,
> turning now, swallowing.

Over the course of the poem, the poet's voice gradually merges into that of the suicides, of the waxwings into which their souls have escaped. The birds fly through the 'whole healing silence of the air' and the shifting, wandering existence of the waxwings gives the souls their final wish:

> to be alive in secret, this is what
> we wanted.

I finally found Peretz's warren of huts and cabins and interviewed him – lean, scarred, hieroglyphed with tattoos – over vodka and greasy *salo*. In the background I could hear the heavy ululations of someone coming off *krokodil*, a vicious heroin-substitute. We spoke about God and drugs and waxwings, which he said were his favourite bird. When we'd finished, I made my way back to the literary festival in darkness, pausing for a moment beneath the empty rowan tree. Later, in the dining room of the Siberia Hotel, I told Dmitry Kuzmin, a well-known Russian poet who was sitting at my table, about the birds I'd seen out by the station yard. He asked me if I'd read Velimir Khlebnikov.

Khlebnikov was one of Russia's great nature poets, a founder of the Hylaea Futurist movement who was described by his collaborator and confidant Mayakovsky as both 'impossible to read' and 'the King of Russian poetry'. When he died – he was only thirty-six – in a remote Novgorod village in 1922, most of his work remained unpublished. He was neglected during the Soviet era, his work dismissed as 'ideologically unsound', too difficult to appeal to the committees and apparatchiks. When editions of his poems were published – in 1940 and 1960 – they were prefaced with warnings that the poet 'did not fully understand the revolution'. It was his unique voice, the genuinely radical approach that Khlebnikov took to language in his poems, that explained both his troubles with the philistine authorities at home and his obscurity abroad. His poems, which are dense and shot-through with neologisms, are incredibly difficult to translate, but slowly he is being recognised as a poet of extravagant, extraordinary gifts, and a visionary writer of the natural world.[8]

Khlebnikov was born in Astrakhan province, down where the Volga enters the Caspian Sea. His first publication was a pamphlet describing the calls of the birds of the Astrakhan Nature Reserve, and the birds of the Volga delta continued to call throughout his poetry, even when he moved first to Kazan, then St Petersburg, then Moscow. He sought to transcribe birdsong, to find a poetic voice as vivid and varied as those of the birds of his childhood. The critic Aleksander Ilichevsky writes that:

Khlebnikov was mathematically precise in his *zaumi*,[9] organising it ... with an ultra-real algebra of song, as powerful in effect as it is

inaccessible . . . Khlebnikov's sound-meanings . . . are a highly precise
transcription of bird-thought, bird-history and bird-drama. During this
process there is a repeated attempt to reveal the main secret of language:
the identification of a medium between the sense, which appears as
one's consciousness is expressed, and the sound-form of the words which
develop this sense in the consciousness of the listener.[10]

In 'Where the Waxwings Used to Dwell', Khlebnikov calls upon the birds
of his memory, writing of the way birds mark the passing of time, how we can
travel down birdsong into our own pasts. T.S. Eliot said that 'Genuine poetry
can communicate before it is understood';[11] no truer than in this poem by
Khlebnikov.[12] It works on us in subterranean ways through its rhythms, its
images, its host of neologisms. In places the poem strays dangerously close
to nonsense verse, but manages to mint from the particulars of its birdworld
a sense of universal nostalgia, a hymn to birdsong that is moving, joyful, and
filled with light:

> Where the waxwings used to dwell,
> Where the pine trees softly swayed,
> A flock of airy momentwills[13]
> Flew around and flew away.
> Where the pine trees softly whooshed
> Where the warblewings sang out
> A flock of airy momentwills
> Flew around and flew about.
> In wild and shadowy disarray
> Among the ghosts of bygone days,
> Wheeled and tintinnabulated.
> A flock of airy momentwills
> A flock of airy momentwills!
> You're warblewingish and beguilish,
> You besot my soul like strumming,
> Like a wave invade my heart!

Go on, ringing warblewings,
Long live airy momentwills!

After the 1917 revolution, Khlebnikov travelled wildly and widely across Russia, collecting bird sounds, experiences, impressions, all of which he recorded in his poetry and journals. He was 'hungry for space', he said, and joined up with the Red Army to support the Jungle Movement of Gilan, a socialist faction seeking to overthrow the Shah of Iran.[14] The revolt ended in failure and Khlebnikov returned to Moscow, hoping to find a publisher for his poems. He failed, ran short of money, became ill. All the time he was working on an over-arching philosophy of history, trying to prove that events were predestined, that war was avoidable, the future brightly hued. In May, 1922, he set out for Novgorod with his friend, the artist Peter Miturich. He died, destitute, largely unmourned, at the end of June.

Now, ninety-four years later, I read Khlebnikov's words and they work upon me like a memory-laden scent, like birdsong, bringing hard before me all the unremembered things of that snowy Siberian afternoon: waxwings and the emptiness of the rowan without them, pale light on pine trees, the cut of vodka through *salo,* the blue sound of a train whistle in the gloaming, and all the cold wide beauty of Russia.

COLLARED DOVE

I CAME UP OUT OF the tube at Stepney Green into the warm sooty air of an early summer evening. I was running late: we were off to the première of a film my sister had made and my father was already there, on the pavement with my brother and some old friends. It took me a few moments to realise something was wrong, a fissure opening before us. I looked at my dad once, then again. He was off-kilter, listing somehow, his eyes drawn downwards. I held out my arms to him and he came and leant against me. I felt the extraordinary weight of him, more weight than mere flesh would account for, as we hobbled to the kerb. My brother hailed a taxi and we took him to the Royal London Hospital.

I'd spent that day pacing the airy ziggurats of Rowley Way, surprising pigeons in the stairwells of the Abbey Road estate. It was the general election of 2015 and I was knocking on doors for Tulip Siddiq, trying to chase out the last few supporters in a race that appeared suddenly closer than we'd thought. I was still wearing my *Vote Labour!* badges as we stumbled into the hospital, where my father was eased into a wheelchair. There were tests, and waiting, and finally the bad news. The bloating in my father's stomach, which his GP had written off as wind, was lymphoma, a tumour the size of a dove, nesting inside.

A few days later, I drove him up to his cottage in Aldeburgh and helped him into bed in his room overlooking the sea. These reversals either slink up on a life gradually, or strike unexpectedly[1] – 'like a sparrowhawk / Screeching after a horror-struck collared-dove / That flails in front of her executioner.'[2] My dad was seventy-seven, but he'd been working – he is a flying instructor – and had seemed untouchable, indestructible, decades from death. Now, tucking a sheet beneath his chin, I watched him slide down into an exhausted sleep. I stood over him for a while, then crossed to the window and saw, there on the roof of the holiday cottage beside his house, a pair of collared doves.

Collared doves were almost unknown in Britain until the 1950s. They were a bird of the Near East, a dusky desert crooner that cooed in the pages of the Arabian Nights. In Mahmoud Darwish's 'The Damascene Collar of the Dove', he writes:

> In Damascus,
> the doves fly
> behind the silk fence
> two . . .
> by two . . .

It is a collared dove that the wily younger brother, Rushdi, in Naguib Mahfouz's *Khan al-Khalili* employs as a medium in his courtship of a local girl, the Cairo equivalent of John Donne's flea:

> Looking up at the dove, he said, 'Good evening, my little dove!' all the while glancing at the girl. He smiled as he noticed her sneak a quick look at the dove. 'What a lovely colour you have,' he went on. 'A brown that is so attractive and charming. Do you know the song "O my tan beauty, my life in tawny hues"?' The girl was listening closely to what he was saying, although she pretended not to.

In the middle years of the last century, the collared dove, which was once prized in aristocratic English dovecots as a specimen of rare exoticism, spread more swiftly through Europe than any other bird on record. In *Birds Brittanica,* Mark Cocker and Richard Mabey propose that the dove's rapacious colonisation of Western and Northern Europe may have been fall-out from the break-up of the Ottoman Empire.[3] They even suggest the doves might have benefitted from wartime environmental dislocations:

> It is a striking irony that the archetypal symbol of peace achieved much of its territorial expansion during the Second World War. Sometimes the dove's movements closely shadowed those of the German panzers. In 1940 it arrived in Poland ... within a decade it had reached the edge of continental Europe and was poised to cross the Channel.

My father lay in bed, riding out the miseries of his months of chemotherapy, and as he lay, he watched the doves build their haphazard nest in the chimney next door. I tried to call him every day, I'd send him poems harvested from my notebooks (mostly about doves). My father would tell me about the birds' progress over the phone, or he'd reply to my poems with emails about the 'old man' of Crabbe Street and his 'pet doves'. He was worried about the birds, he wrote, about the flimsiness of their nest, the precariousness of their existence: 'Too perilous, too porous, too uncomfortable and too small, decides the old man. It can't serve. Not for one bird, let alone two. Not for an egg, however small.'

We spoke about the doves, about poetry, to avoid speaking about other things, or rather, as a way of speaking about them undangerously. I remember my father calling me in a panic on a night of high winds. I told him how the doves had spread across Europe, across America, how a little wind wouldn't stand in the way of their wild proliferation. Sure enough, the birds, dun and doughty, sat on. The doves were his companions when his children couldn't be there beside him. 'The old man rarely speaks to the sitting bird out loud,' he wrote to me late one night. 'Obvious danger of perceived dementia persuades him to whisper, to rely on thought transference. He likes to think he is understood, maybe detecting interest from the occasional: "Coo-coo".'

Time passed, the incubation continued: incubate, to lie upon. My father slept late, took long naps, and within him the tumour – which the chemo-therapy had shrunken to the size of an egg – waited. Whenever we spoke of the birds, I'd call to mind a quote from Shakespeare's *Venus and Adonis*: 'Two strengthless doves will draw me through the sky.' I needed those placid, unheroic doves to do what I could not: to get my father airborne again.[4]

In Eliot's *Four Quartets*, it's the dove in 'Little Gidding' that brings the cycle to an end, just as the singing of the thrush in 'Burnt Norton' initiates the sequence. My father, an atheist, didn't like Eliot's doves (although he enjoyed Stravinsky's setting of the lines to music). He found them theatrical and delusory, the superstitious co-opting of the real bird into a mere symbol. The dove of 'Little Gidding', written when Eliot himself was recuperating from illness, is a violent Pentecostal bird, a vengeful spirit come to shrive the earth through fire:

> The dove descending breaks the air
> With flame of incandescent terror
> Of which the tongues declare
> The one discharge from sin and error.
> The only hope, or else despair
> Lies in the choice of pyre or pyre-
> To be redeemed from fire by fire.

I love to imagine Eliot, though, fire-watching during the Blitz on the red rooftops of Bloomsbury, flames pluming in the distance. The dove here links German bombs to the cleansing fire of the Holy Spirit and draws us back to the beginning of the sequence of poems.[5] It also acts as a herald of the unnamed ghost – Yeats? Swift? – whom Eliot meets walking through the rubble.

> After the dark dove with the flickering tongue
> Had passed below the horizon of his homing
> While the dead leaves still rattled on like tin
> Over the asphalt where no other sound was
> Between three districts whence the smoke arose
> I met one walking, loitering and hurried

As if blown towards me like the metal leaves
Before the urban dawn wind unresisting.

Wallace Stevens was another for whom the dove carried complex symbolic meaning. His North American dove was almost certainly the mourning dove, but Stevens's is a bird so deeply entwined with its literary and scriptural forebears that it might be the gentler brother of Eliot's fire-breather.[6] In 'The Dove in the Belly', the bird is at once a representation of religious feeling and creative inspiration: 'The dove builds his nest and coos' for 'the whole of appearance'. It is also Venus's bird, a fecund spirit out of whom pours all of creation, and all of the words to tell it.[7] The simple beauty of Stevens's questioning nature poem builds into the final, rousing lines, which call people to seek out the dove within, to find comfort in it:

And the people in costumes,
Though poor, though raggeder than ruin, have that
Within them right for terraces—oh, brave salut!
Deep dove, placate you in your hiddenness.

My father's doves hatched a pair of scrawny, fluffy chicks: 'One day the old man sees a lump move,' he wrote to me in August.[8] 'There's life. He's overjoyed. Mostly he sees beaks, opened wide: two, jostling for attention. The rate at which they grow defies belief. Parents are attentive but pickings are scarce. Yet two beaks rapidly develop into chicks that again put nest to test.' For my dad, chemotherapy, with its hair loss and ritual cleansing, segued into the nausea and exhaustion of radiotherapy.

More time passed, my father's life strung out between his bed and the hospital. Early one morning, he was woken by a noise. In the first light of dawn, his eyes opened to one of the fledgling doves, flapping on his windowsill. His email – long, joyful – came through that evening.

'Drawing the curtain back has an unexpected effect,' he wrote.

She looks up and back at him and stops flapping. He can't deny that faith and trust enter the scene. How else explain what occurs next? He opens the window with his left hand. The squeak of the un-oiled catch doesn't disturb her as she rests, trusting. This is the moment the old man fears, certain she'll struggle as he tries to guide her to her escape. This is not what happens.

Placid and accepting, she allows his right hand to embrace her whole body from underneath while he emanates all he can in telepathic sedation. It, or something like it, must be working, for her wings remain static and spread, her breast neither heaving nor fluttering. She holds him in a trusting gaze. Is this to be believed? How warm to the touch. He wants to stretch the moment to eternity.

Not until the old man raises his arm, as if launching a kite on the beach, does she show willing to depart. Even now she allows herself a swooping descent, as part of the launch, before strong symmetrical beats of her wings overcome gravity and she reaches for the sky.

The cancer is smaller now, only visible under the radioactive light of certain scanners, where the tumour glows like a gem. We wait. The doves have built a new nest for a new year, in the cottage by the sea. My father listens to them cooing. He insists that he doesn't hear the melancholy note in their voice.[9] I think for a while before sending him 'Listening to Collared Doves' by E.J. Scovell, which I find in Simon Armitage and Tim Dee's anthology, *The Poetry of Birds*. It's a lovely poem, but it scarcely fits with the optimistic veneer we, as a family, have painted over everything during the dark year of our dad's illness. My father reads it and asks for a copy of Armitage and Dee's anthology, which I send him, along with the wonderful Carcanet Press edition of Scovell's *Collected Poems*. He responds with a final thought from the old man of Aldeburgh:

This morning, the old man drew back the curtains in the spare room to hear a frantic scuffling from the window box of which a tiny corner was caught by the sun. Two collared doves flapped away, almost diaphanous, climbing up in the beam of light.[10] They haunt the place, as if nostalgic, like Scovell herself.

I am homesick now for middle age, as then
For youth. For youth is our home-land: we were born
And lived there long, though afterwards moved on
From state to state, too slowly acclimatising
Perhaps and never fluent, through the surprising
Countries, in any languages but one.

This mourning now for middle age, no more
For youth, confirms me old as not before.
Age rounds the world, they say, to childhood's far
Archaic shores; it may be so at last,
But what now (strength apart) I miss the most
Is time unseen like air, since everywhere.

And yet, when in the months and in the skies
That were the cuckoos', and in the nearer trees
That were the deep-voiced wood-pigeons', it is
Instead now the collared doves that call and call
(Their three flat notes growing traditional),
I think we live long enough, listening to these.

I draw my line out from their simple curve
And say, our natural span may be enough;
And think of one I knew and her long life;
And how the climate changed and how the sign-
Posts changed, defaced, from her Victorian
Childhood and youth, through our century of grief,

And how she adapted as she could, not one
By nature adaptable, bred puritan
(Though quick to be pleased and having still her own
Lightness of heart). She died twenty years ago,
Aged, of life – it seems, all she could do
Having done, all the change that she could know having known.

SNOW GOOSE

I'VE NEVER SEEN A wild snow goose, but I feel their presence in the familiar sight of greylag and barnacle geese barrelling in from the North Sea to land on the marshes at Minsmere in Suffolk: the sense that these birds have witnessed unpeopled landscapes of crags and gullies, taiga and tundra, wolf-haunted forests and polar ice-floes. Michael Longley hears these whispers of wild elsewheres in the sound of distant geese, summoning before him wide skies and sunlight on snow.[1] His geese are:

> So far away as to be almost absent
> And yet so many of them we can hear
> The line of snow geese along the horizon.

The voices of the forty thousand birds 'Tell me about cranberry fields, the harvest / Floating on flood water, acres of crimson.' The geese are envoys from lands we'll never see and, through the birds, Longley can roam to the end of the world to pick cranberries for his lover.

Geese passing over, particularly at night, when they appear dimly luminous, like searchlights on the bellies of clouds, gives me a delicious shiver, their voices the foghorns of ghost ships. In 'Skeins o Geese', written in Scots dialect, Kathleen Jamie asks:

Whit dae birds write on the dusk?
A word never spoken or read.
The skeins turn hame,
on the wind's dumb moan, a soun,
maybe human, bereft.

Mary Oliver wrote two exquisite poems about the sight of geese flying above. The first is 'Snow Geese', with its opening a hymn to the fleeting beauty of birds: 'Oh, to love what is lovely, and will not last!' Oliver's snow geese shimmer, taking on the colours of the landscape around them, of the long northern rays of the sun: 'being the color of snow, catching the sun / so they were, in part at least, golden.' Time stops for Oliver as she looks up at them, and then they're gone, and from their passing comes a lesson about the good things that touch our lives and how we mustn't try to hold on to them, but be thankful we've shared the world with such beauty, such birds.

What matters
is that, when I saw them,
I saw them
as through the veil, secretly, joyfully, clearly.

My favourite of Oliver's poems is 'Wild Geese'. The freedom of the birds flying overhead offers both a challenge and a dispensation to those below; the wide emptiness of the American landscape is revealed, offered to the speaker (and the spoken-to), liberating them from whatever prison they've built around them. It's a poem which flirts with sentimentality, and yet there is such sincerity, such wisdom, that I can't read it aloud without my voice catching on something sharp and snapping a little on those rousing final lines:

You do not have to be good.
You do not have to walk on your knees
for a hundred miles through the desert repenting.

You only have to let the soft animal of your body
    love what it loves.
Tell me about despair, yours, and I will tell you mine.
Meanwhile the world goes on.
Meanwhile the sun and the clear pebbles of the rain
are moving across the landscapes,
over the prairies and the deep trees,
the mountains and the rivers.
Meanwhile the wild geese, high in the clean blue air,
are heading home again.
Whoever you are, no matter how lonely,
the world offers itself to your imagination,
calls to you like the wild geese, harsh and exciting –
over and over announcing your place
in the family of things.

The best that literature can do is to let us feel known. With Mary Oliver in the world, we ought all to feel a little less lonely, her words a permission slip that we might be something closer to our true selves, less burdened by the weight of our own personal weirdnesses. My two volumes of her *New and Selected Poems* are thumb-grubby and tattered, favourite pages slip from broken spines. I must have copied the majority of her poems into my notebooks over the years since I discovered her fifth, Pulitzer Prize-winning collection *American Primitive*, in a second-hand bookshop in Brighton some time in the late 1990s. It's hard to think of two poets less alike than Mary Oliver and Ted Hughes – they shine with such different lights – but I don't think I'd have written this book, or loved birds as much, without them both.

William Fiennes's first book, *The Snow Geese*, told of how, in his early twenties, he found himself hospitalised with an unnamed disease and became obsessed with a novella and the bird in it.[2] The book was *The Snow Goose* by Paul Gallico, which I remember reading in a single sitting in Worthing Library one rainy childhood Saturday afternoon. My legs weren't long enough to touch the floor, but even then I was struck by the battle between sincerity and schmaltz that rumbled across its pages. 'Something in the story haunted me,' Fiennes writes in his book, and Gallico's parable has stayed with me too, that brief, sentimental tale of a man, a girl and a goose in the early years of the Second World War.

I'm still not sure whether to laugh or cry at the book's end, when the snow goose – *La Princesse Perdue* – returns from Philip Rhayader's doomed mission to Dunkirk. Fritha, the young Saxon girl, is at the lighthouse tending the geese when she:

> came running to the sea wall and turned her eyes, not toward the distant Channel whence a sail might come, but in the sky from whose flaming arches plummeted the snow goose. Then the sight, the sound, and the solitude surrounding broke the dam within her and released the surging, overwhelming truth of her love, let it well forth in tears.
>
> Wild spirit called to wild spirit, and she seemed to be flying with the great bird, soaring with it in the evening sky and hearkening to Rhayader's message.
>
> Sky and earth were trembling with it and filled her beyond the bearing of it, 'Frith! Fritha! Frith, my love. Good-bye, my love.' The white pinions, black-tipped, were beating it out upon her heart, and her heart was answering: 'Philip, I love 'ee.'

The story stirred in Fiennes – lonely and sickly – a feeling of *Fernweh*, an obscure restlessness; in his *The Snow Geese*, he writes that he couldn't stop thinking about:

> the wintry, laundered freshness of white plumage immediately after moult; the dense, lacquer-black eyes that glinted like china beads; the wing bedlam of flocks rising from marshland roosts. I was drawn to these images. I felt shackled, cooped-up. It was as if I'd glimpsed birds through the high, barred window of a cell. Day by day, my restlessness increased.

He set out to follow the birds from their wintering-grounds on the plains of Texas, up through the empty flatlands of the mid-West, across Canada to Hudson Bay and then onwards to the Ultima Thule of Foxe Land, Baffin Island, where the geese spent the long summers and white nights. On Greyhound buses, pick-up trucks and boats, he headed 'north with the snow geese, complicit with birds'.

The book is full of the most extraordinary, new-minted writing. The sound of the birds at sundown is that of 'a marina, of halliards flicking on metal masts'. Birds arrive on a lake and it's 'a diaspora in reverse'. Fiennes's prose seems to teach new ways of seeing. His geese are vividly alive, totally real. They:

> flew from the south in long skeins and echelons that crossed and undulated, or appeared, by a trick of angle and distance, to twirl in ropes and double helixes. Geese flew in their limited alphabet of Vs, Js and Ws, or in interlocking chevrons like the insignia on officers' epaulettes, and the high raillery of snow geese in flight made a descant to the deeper, rougher honking of Canada geese roosting in the phragmites and cattail.

Everything is rendered with beautiful precision, so that *The Snow Geese* becomes less a book about birds, more a paean to the redemptive power of close looking and the dignity conferred by naming – 'a method of noticing,' Fiennes says at one point. 'It seemed that what a thing was called was part of what it looked like.'

We find him returning home at the end of the book with a new spring in his step, swallows flitting around him. As *La Princesse Perdue* had helped build Rhayader's strength for his heroics at Dunkirk, Fiennes's geese, in their dappled multitudes, offered a way out of the slough he'd fallen into. It may be that, in the overwhelming strictures of the snow geese migration, we find mirrored the less visible cares of our own life's journey, that from these birds who've been through everything and pressed on, we can draw some bravery.[3]

BARN OWL

Y OU DON'T WATCH BARN owls, you encounter them. It was a cold, clear February afternoon and Neil and I were walking back from Camber Castle across the mudflats of Rye Harbour Nature Reserve. It was not long after we'd decided to write this book together and there was a special new intimacy between us, as if we were both privy to a happy secret – a pregnancy, perhaps. The sun had just gone down behind us, turning the sky vermillion, and it was as if the winter world were celebrating too. In front, in the gloaming, there rose from the reeds a puff of smoke, a wraith, a bird paler than any living thing has a right to be. She glided ahead of us, luminous in the dim light, and wheeled to perch on a fence-post, hanging in the air for a long moment before settling, wings spread.[1] She regarded us coolly and then set off again, an alien ship drifting over the earth. Neil and I stood, bewitched, until the barn owl disappeared, embowered in a clasp of willow. We celebrated all the way to the car.

Richard Mabey's writing has illuminated my path back to birds, as you'll have gathered from the number of times he appears in this book. With a joyful eccentricity of vision and rigorously precise language, Mabey shapes the British landscape and the birds that fly above it. It's profoundly political nature writing, radical in the vein of Hazlitt and Cobbett, full of righteous anger at the depredations wrought on the natural world by unthinking humanity. It's also wonderfully stylish prose, bringing the birds and flowers he describes to startling life, and my most recent notebooks are crammed with Mabey's work.

He writes beautifully about barn owls, following in the footsteps of his literary forefather, Gilbert White.[2] There's something tragic about Mabey's white owls, as if they're the ghosts of a vanishing Britain, wilder and more magical. In one essay on the bird, he notes how, despite the uncanny folklore surrounding them, barn owls have always lived close to mankind.[3]

> I cannot recall ever seeing one more than a few hundred yards from a village or human settlement. They haunt the roughest, oldest edges of the parish landscape – the green lanes and stackyards and hedgebanks – and with those open, inquisitive faces that look as if they are mounted directly on to the wings, seem like guardian spirits, patrollers of the bounds.[4]

That mournful note played again in *Nature Cure*, Mabey's memoir about how love and wildlife dragged him out of a devastating depression. The loss of barn owls – both the bird's decline and the fact that he's had to move to an apparently owl-less East Anglia – is a deep wound.[5] The barn owls draw him down into childhood, and his pursuit of them becomes part of a wider search for the playful, curious, eager self he'd lost somewhere in the middle of his life's path.

> Up till fifty years ago they'd been parish familiars throughout England, keeping their pale vigil over the pastures. When I was a child a pair had nested in a barn not more than 300 yards from my house, and their hunting range matched up almost exactly with the boundaries of our gang's territory in the Field: over the old brick piles that were all that remained of the Hall, up the ivy-clad wall that lined the council estate, across the steep field we used for tobogganing, then down, if we were lucky, through the bosky edges of our back gardens. The memory of the owls beating past the poplar trees – burnished golden wings against

lime-green leaves in the evening light – is one of the few visual images of childhood I can recall with absolute clarity. Now I see the white owl not so much as an object in the landscape but as a creature looking at me.

Barn owls seem so heavily freighted with meaning and myth that they live mostly in the realm of symbol, with just one talon in the natural world. It was this mythical aspect of the owl that was part of the enchantment of two of the books I loved as a child and which my children now love in turn. The first is *The Owl Service* by Alan Garner, in which Alison's folded paper owls dredge up ancient myths from the Welsh countryside. There's also *Titus Groan* by Mervyn Peake, in which the Lord Sepulchrave, driven mad by the burning of his beloved library, believes himself to be an owl. He retreats into the crepuscular world of the Tower of Flints:

> This tower, patched unevenly with black ivy, arose like a mutilated finger from among the fists of knuckled masonry and pointed blasphemously at heaven. At night the owls made of it an echoing throat; by day it stood voiceless and cast its long shadow.

Finally, he is torn apart by the ravenous owls.

Virginia Woolf said that Roger Fry disdained 'the village churchyard, with its owls, its epitaphs and its ivy', and the owl has become a shorthand for the gothic, the uncanny. Gray's country graveyard wouldn't have been the same without its owl:

> from yonder ivy-mantled tower
> The moping owl does to the moon complain
> Of such as, wandering near her secret bower,
> Molest her ancient solitary reign.

Baudelaire's churchyard owls sit in yew, rather than ivy, but the atmosphere is the same: the owls are discontented, mean, melancholy:

Within the shelter of black yews
The owls in ranks are ranged apart
Like foreign gods, whose eyeballs dart
Red fire. They meditate and muse.[6]

R.S. Thomas also situates his owl in a graveyard, although this one's more like a medium between the human and the supernatural:

a pale
face hovering in the afterdraught
of the spirit ... It is the breath
of the churchyard.[7]

Chaucer makes the link more directly, calling it 'the owl which announces death'.

It is perhaps because the barn owl has become so mythical, so un-natural, that Mabey and others have felt compelled to describe them so precisely, recovering them a little from their symbolic appropriation by literature, art and film. There are dozens of encounters with barn owls in Mabey's work. He wrote in a *New Statesman* article about 'dousing' for barn owls – looking for likely spots on Ordinance Survey maps and waiting for the birds to arrive. Sure enough, on the occasion he describes, one February afternoon near Cookley in Suffolk ...

It came very close and I could see the individual scroll and lozenge markings on its wings. A dark bird, so probably a female ... Ten minutes later, a paler bird (perhaps her mate) drifted out of a thicket in my direction. It was a fly-past.

These 'fly-pasts' are one of the crutches Mabey reaches out for in his despondency. It was the same for J.A. Baker, another solitary, unhappy man who felt a particular connection to the ghostly white owl. This passage, from his lesser-known *The Hill of Summer*, an account of the progress of one summer across the South of England, is luminous, voluptuous and does what all the best nature writing does: becomes an immediate and central part of the collage of cultural sources through which we view the world. I am ravished every time by that 'fading giraffe skins of light and shade':

> There is a sudden haunting whiteness to the south. It seems to hover on the shining surface of the sea. Then it descends, and comes closer. It is a barn owl. He glows in the last sunlight, like burning snow, a white incandescence casting a black shadow. He flies quickly through the cooling dusk of the fields, and his whiteness is strangely difficult to follow. Some of his owl-shape seems to ebb away into the ambient air. He turns in the darkness of an oak, and floats forward over the fading giraffe-skins of light and shade that still dapple the sunlit field... The broad head looks down, hanging like the globe of a giant puff-ball below the moth-like fanning of the wings. The soft ear-coverts lift in a wind of sound, and the cavernous ears beneath them echo with the endless rustling of the running mice. The white facial disc of the barn owl is a corolla of shining feathers, a radiance of petals that beams the diminishing light down to the dark-channelled calyces of the owl's huge Lebanon eyes.

There's a deep affinity between barn owls and rivers. Practically, it's the water-voles that bring them to the banks, but the sight of an owl drifting over the misty surface of a river is one of the timeless images of the British countryside so that, as you watch, you feel Bede and Boudicca, Chaucer and Langman, King Arthur and Prince Hal standing beside you, and time drops away until it's just you and the bird wafting through the air above the water.

Olivia Laing wrote of the Ouse in her first book, *To the River*. It was here that Virginia Woolf tied on her hat, filled her pockets with rocks and stepped into the water, and Laing walks the length of the river in an attempt to fend off her own megrims.[8] Owls keep her company on her quest:

On autumn evenings I've often watched a barn owl here, quartering the field, and once I startled it face on. It was dusk, a moon three days before full caught just above the treeline. The owl took a rough zigzagging path up the meadow, hovered a beat or two, and came to within ten feet of where I stood. Then it paused, and the full intent stare of that tiny, ghostly face rested upon me, until it registered what it was looking at and with silent, smoke-gold wings flew on.

In *The Outrun*, another book about recovery, Amy Liptrot returns from a dissolute, drug-and-alcohol-raddled existence in Hackney to rebuild her life on the rocky and wind-blown Orkneys, where she grew up. Over the course of the book, Liptrot sloughs off her London self, sinking deeper into the landscape around her. Her recuperation is aided by a series of sublime encounters – with the icy sea, with the Northern Lights, with an owl:[9]

> There are wonderful moments. I make eye contact with a short-eared owl, plentiful this year and known locally as 'catty faces.' It's on a fence post next to where I park, and we both turn our heads and see each other. I gasp, the owl flies. One still-pink dawn, just before summer, I stop at the Ring of Brodgar on the way home. There's no one around, and I take all my clothes off and run around the Neolithic stone circle.

Dusk. What the poet John Hollander calls 'owl-light – in the time between / Dog and wolf'.[10] It was September 2016, the Kent/Sussex border, deep in a fierce Indian summer, everything sighing into night as the heat left the land. I was running, as I ran most nights, down to the river. The last traces of daylight were draping themselves over the hills, but in the valley, where I was headed, all was dim and rich and purple. I made my way through woods, along a rough track and then out into a field of flax – in daylight, there were skylarks here – and down to the river. The banks were high and I lowered myself through the reeds to where a small lip of tussocky earth hung out over the water. With a quick check of the path behind me, I stripped off my clothes and let myself down into the cool dark river.

I swam upstream a little, towards the castle, and then lay back, star-shaped, and let myself drift in the slow current, through misty emanations, past a willow that leant over the water, stirring the surface with its branches. There was a perturbation of the mist, a brief hiss, and then I saw her, the barn owl looming low along the water towards me, until she was over me, her soft white belly almost touching mine. She caught sight of me at the last moment and sheared up into a willow, where I saw her, watching me, goblin-eyes green and luminous in the dusk.

She went ahead of me like a lantern as I made my way home, drifting low over the fields. She left me just before I reached the lit windows of the first farmhouse of the village, wheeling off into the trees, and I sent my prayers with her, this ghost-bird. On my way back, through woods where I ran with my arms outstretched, memory leading me, it hit me: how much of who I was now rested on encounters like this, on the secret friendship of birds.

NIGHTINGALE

THIS BOOK CAME TO me in a cabin in the woods. The cabin sat in a clearing overlooking an inlet of Lake Oconee, twenty miles south of Athens, Georgia. I was up before dawn, out on the stoop in a rocking chair watching the sky fill with milky light, the fish rising, a blue heron beating his way lazily across the surface of the lake. Circumspect deer trotted past, following their wet black noses. An American kestrel was hovering over the old oaks on the opposite shore and, in the visionary light of that Southern morning, Gerard Manley Hopkins came and stood beside me. He was a wreck of a priest, ancient at forty, bleary-eyed and apologetic. 'I CAUGHT this morning morning's minion, king- / dom of daylight's dauphin, dapple-dawn-drawn Falcon,' he whispered to me in his ruined ghost-voice.

It has taken me a little over eighteen months to pull all this together, fishing out material from twenty-five years of notes. Deep in the middle of the writing, we decided to move our home from London to Kent (the book, the birds, at least partly responsible, the wish to live a cleaner life). I now lie in bed and hear nightingales when I wake in the small darkness, rather than the shriek of sirens on the Harrow Road. I listen to those eloquent migrants, who spend only a quarter of their lives in the UK, and I think of others braving the roiling waters of the Mediterranean, looking for kinder country.[1] I think of W.H. Davies, addressing:

You Nightingales, that came so far,
From Afric's shore;
With these rich notes, unloaded now
Against my door.

It's not an easy time to be English. Sudden fissures have appeared in the landscape, old wounds reopened, a bubbling intransitive rage permeates the air, down here close to the ports, to the faded resorts where the people brew and fulminate. I'd thought that this act of personal archaeology – my return to birds – would be a small thing, a distraction from Brexit and belligerent nationalism. Now I'm not so sure. Michael Longley said that nature was a way into, rather than an escape from, politics. 'My nature writing is my most political . . . I want the light from Carrigskeewaun to irradiate the northern darkness,' he wrote. 'Describing the world in a meticulous way is a consecration and a stay against damaging dogmatism.'[2]

I wanted the nightingale to be the last chapter in this book precisely because the bird seems to live trapped, trembling, between the page and the sky. Poets have broken themselves, and their language, trying to express in words the eternal moment, always dissolving, of the nightingale's song. There is a nobility in this struggle, to *make new* a creature that has become a trope, more fable than bird. In our age of great lies and slippery truths, attempting the accurate expression of something as pure, as unpartisan, as a nightingale's song is a political act. Anna Akhmatova, the greatest Russian poet of the twentieth century, found in the silent nightingale the perfect metaphor for writing under the pall of state censorship:

As a silver, delicate strand
Is woven in my dark tresses –
Only you, silent nightingale,
Can understand this torment.[3]

Mahmoud Darwish called up the nightingale again and again in his work as a symbol of the liberated poetic spirit. In 'Diary of a Palestinian Wound', he says that through suffering, 'we came to know what makes the voice of the nightingale / a dagger shining in the face of the invaders.' In *Defiance*, he writes of the power of poetry to speak within the torture chamber, to assert itself against the violent impositions of his captors. The poem ends with the burning image of the unquenchable nightingale, singing:

Under the whip –
Under the chains –
In spite of my handcuffs
I have a million nightingales
On the branches of my heart
Singing the song of liberation.

This vision of the incarcerated poet listening to the free rush of the nightingale's song is picked up in an icy prose poem by Tomas Tranströmer, the Swedish Nobel laureate.

In the green midnight at the nightingale's northern limit. Heavy leaves hang in trance, the deaf cars race towards the neon-line. The nightingale's voice rises without wavering to the side, it is as penetrating as a cock-crow, but beautiful and free of vanity. I was in prison and it visited me. I was sick and it visited me. I didn't notice it then, but I do now. Time streams down from the sun and the moon and into all the tick-tock-thankful clocks. But right here there is no time. Only the nightingale's voice, the raw resonant notes that whet the night sky's gleaming scythe.[4]

I have filled a notebook with my own attempts to snare the nightingale's voice in words. I try to throw the net of language over the song, but it pours through, laughing when I call it *ecstatic* and *riotous* and *lyrical* and *otherworldly*.[5] In an essay on the nightingales of Tuscany, D.H. Lawrence wrote of the way poets have tried (and failed) to translate the bird's song into theirs. 'Jug-jug-jug! say the medieval writers, to represent the rolling of the little balls of lightning in the nightingale's throat. A wild rich sound, richer than the eyes in a peacock's tail.' John Clare attempted seriously, joyfully, to 'syllable the sounds' after hearing a bird in the apple tree outside his window in May 1832.[6] The transcription was worked into a delightful poem, 'The Nightingale', which you cannot read aloud without a grin on your face and a rising heart.

> 'Chew-chew chew-chew' and higher still,
> 'Cheer-cheer cheer-cheer' more loud and shrill,
> 'Cheer-up cheer-up cheer-up'—and dropped
> Low—'Tweet tweet jug jug jug'—and stopped
> One moment just to drink the sound
> Her music made, and then a round
> Of stranger witching notes was heard
> As if it was a stranger bird:
> 'Wew-wew wew-wew chur-chur chur-chur
> Woo-it woo-it'—could this be her?
> 'Tee-rew tee-rew tee-rew tee-rew
> Chew-rit chew-rit'—and ever new—
> 'Will-will will-will grig-grig grig-grig.'

It's not just poets who've wrestled with the nightingale's immoderate choiring. In his *Catalogue d'oiseaux*, composed in 1958, Olivier Messiaen tried to capture the torrent of a nightingale's song in music. He described the piece in a television lecture recorded in the 1970s:

> And here is the nightingale, who bursts into song all of a sudden. The second verse, that's the percussion, consists of two legendary sounds. Koo-tsee-koo-tsee-koo-tsee-koo-tsee-kooo. Then, lower down now, a combination of harpsichord and gong, and it goes choob-choof-choob-choof-choob. Then a series of repeated notes, culminating in a victorious *torculus*[7]: kyo-kyo-kyo-kyo-kyo-kyo-labaryx! And finally, the slow, distant, lunar sounds, as if coming down to us from another planet, with

the bird departed far, far, far away, and then he's right there in a flurry, with his wild, rapid, strident finale.[8]

In the song of the nightingale, poets have found reflections of their own internal landscapes, articulating, through nature, old losses, or giving voice to new griefs by yoking them to this ancient, fabled song. In Keats's 'Ode to a Nightingale', the bird itself never really escapes from the artifice of the poem into the world. Even in those final, famous lines – 'Was it a vision, or a waking dream? / Fled is that music: – Do I wake or sleep?' – we remain unsure as to whether the nightingale was ever there, or merely a figment of poetic afflatus.[9] This image of the nightingale as muse is called up in Aristophanes's *The Birds*, first performed in 414 BC:

Tawnythroat, Partner
In song, dark
Muse, dearest of Birds:
Come, let the curving long
Line of your fluting
Fall, sparkling
Undersong to our words.

Shelley also knows the nightingale as the writer's daemon, his familiar. We become the perfect audience when a nightingale sings and the bird's voice, in which there is no subjectivity, no artfulness, but all spirit, is the model of poetic expression.[10] In *A Defence of* Poetry, Shelley says that a:

poet is a nightingale who sits in darkness, and sings to cheer its own solitude with sweet sounds; his auditors are as men entranced by the melody of an unseen musician, who feel they're moved and softened, yet know not whence or why.

I was in Tom Paulin's office, aged nineteen, when the call came through in which he learnt that Ted Hughes had died. His face opened in grief for a few seconds, then he collected himself, replaced the receiver and told me the news. It was a strange situation; I felt the loss deeply myself – Hughes was one of my gods, *Crow* a book I turned to again and again in those messy late-teenage years – but he and Hughes had been friends and I felt as if I was intruding upon a moment of deep, private pain. To remember him, we spoke about his poetry. I'd just finished Hughes's translation of Ovid's *Metamorphoses*, and Paulin and I talked about the myth of Philomela, about how Ovid's dark, violent tale leaps across the centuries, re-accommodating itself to the concerns of each new age. The end of the poem, which tells of two daughters of the King of Athens, and a rape and the murder of a child, subverts our expectations of violent revenge, replacing it with a higher form of justice as Tereus, who 'was the tomb of his boy', and the sisters Philomela and Procne, are transformed into birds:

> And suddenly they were flying. One swerved
> On wings into the forest,
> The other, with the blood still on her breast,
> Flew up under the eaves of the palace.
> And Tereus, charging blind
> In his delirium of grief and vengeance,
> No longer caring what happened –
> He too was suddenly flying.
> . . .
> He had become a hoopoe.
> Philomela
> Mourned in the forest, a nightingale.
> Procne
> Lamented round and round the palace,
> A swallow.[11]

Paulin and I turned to T.S. Eliot's 'The Waste Land' and how it appropriated the myth of Philomela, and how at home the story feels against the backdrop of Eliot's spectral Cityboys and desperate suburbanites, his sham clairvoyants and corrupt public houses:

> Above the antique mantel was displayed
> As though a window gave upon the sylvan scene
> The change of Philomel, by the barbarous king
> So rudely forced; yet there the nightingale
> Filled all the desert with inviolable voice
> And still she cried, and still the world pursues,
> 'Jug Jug' to dirty ears. [12]

The ears of Eliot's motley cast of characters hear the nightingale's voice at its most unlovely. Nothing of the exuberance of Clare's transposition, nor Keats's introverted association with the melancholy bird of poesie, only another reminder of the failure of words to measure up to the nightingale's song. There's also the idea that the way we hear the bird's song says something crucial about who we are.

> Twit twit twit
> Jug jug jug jug jug jug
> So rudely forc'd.
> Tereu[13]

Virginia Woolf uses the same coarse language in *The Waves*, where Jinny identifies herself – beautiful, physical, intuitive – with the nightingale whose fluency she cannot express but in the crudest, human terms: 'Jug, jug, jug. I sing like the nightingale whose melody is crowded in the too narrow passage of her throat.'[14]

Some of us hear only our own sorrows in the nightingale's song. We bring so much of ourselves to the *tabula rasa* of the bird's voice, colonising it with our own crepuscular longings, our losses. In his 'Rossignol', Verlaine hears the nightingale and finds memories 'Swoop among the yellow foliage / Of my heart'. It seems to him that the bird is 'hymning the Absent One' until the nightingale and his lost love become one, all the intricate constellation of feelings crystallised within a stream of song.

> Nothing but the voice – the languishing voice –
> Of the bird that was my Earliest Love,
> Singing still as on that earliest day;
> And in the sad magnificence of a moon
> That rises with pale solemnity, a
> Summer night, heavy and melancholy,
> Full of silence and obscurity,
> Lulls in the sky that a soft wind caresses
> The quivering tree and the weeping bird.[15]

When, in the heart of the wood that sits between my house and the square-towered church, I stop to listen to the nightingale, I'm never sure if I prefer the bird singing or the moments of silence afterwards, when my mind catches up to the song. It's in this silence that I summon what Wallace Stevens calls the 'yellow moon of words about the nightingale / In measureless measures'.[16]

The words bring a richer complexity to the song, acting as this book should, if I've got it even half-right. Every new poem, each luminous piece of nature writing, every well-struck metaphor – bird-writing should build up and brighten birds in our minds, adding new layers of feeling, of understanding, of love. In the silence after the nightingale stops singing, we should hear the words rush in, words that may never quite capture the bird as we know it, but in whose noble failures we find new ways of figuring our world:

> Beneath
> The stillness of everything gone, and being still,
> Being and sitting still, something resides . . .
> And the stillness is in the key, all of it is,
> The stillness is all in the key of that desolate sound.[17]

I'm finishing this book in early autumn, in the rose-clad, red-brick rectory we now call home. The nightingales have all departed, the orchard is heavy with fruit, the first leaves are falling from the old oaks that circle the house like benevolent sentries. The past summer, which has been warm and lived outdoors – in tents, in hammocks, in the garden – I have heard nightingales in deep Wealden hollows and I have been happy. Happy like Christina Rossetti, who found the bird's song heart-repairing, rather than heart-breaking.[18] Happy like Coleridge, who thought that 'In Nature there is nothing melancholy', and the nightingale's reputation for mournfulness was coined by:

> some night-wandering man whose heart was pierced
> With the remembrance of a grievous wrong,
> Or slow distemper, or neglected love.

This 'poor wretch' then 'made all gentle sounds tell back the tale / Of his own sorrow.'

Happy like D.H. Lawrence, whom I hear last, his baffled delight, his beloved Tuscany. Lawrence's nightingale.

> Hello! Hello! Hello! It is the brightest sound, perhaps, of all sounds in the world: a nightingale piping up . . . 'There goes the nightingale!' you say to yourself: and it is as if the stars were darting up from the little thicket and leaping away into the vast vagueness of the sky, to be hidden and gone . . . He is the noisiest, most inconsiderate, most obstreperous and jaunty bird in the whole kingdom of birds. How John Keats managed to begin his 'Ode to a Nightingale' with 'My heart aches and a drowsy numbness pains my senses . . .' – well, I for one don't know. You can hear the nightingale silverily shouting: 'What? What? What, John? Heart aches and a drowsy numbness pains? – tra-la-la!-tri-li-lilly-lilyly!'

ABOUT THE AUTHOR AND ARTIST

Alex Preston is a bestselling and award-winning novelist, most recently of the critically acclaimed *In Love and War*. He appears regularly on BBC television and radio. He writes for *the Telegraph, Harper's Bazaar* and *Town & Country Magazine* as well as monthly fiction reviews for the *Observer*. He is a Senior Lecturer in Creative Writing at the University of Kent.

Neil Gower is an internationally acclaimed artist. His clients include most major publishing houses in the UK & US and magazines such as *The New Yorker, The Economist* and *Vanity Fair*. He has recently completed work on a celebrated new set of covers for Bill Bryson's entire backlist as well as private commissions for Sir Roy Strong and Raymond Blanc.

ARTIST'S NOTE

All my life, I've felt it a blessing to have had the twin complexities of light and the English language at my disposal. Each has proved an infinite source of delight, surprise and inspiration. It is the cocktail of the two that has made collaborating on this book a unique joy. Alex and I fell into the rhythm of him sending me the chapters one by one as he finished them, ink still wet. Every one was simultaneously gift and gauntlet; his fresh words and the timeless words of others the vivid sparks from which I coaxed each bird into flame.

You will find several references here to the South Downs, in the heart of which I live. Much of the inspiration for the paintings came to me during long runs over the ravishing Ravilious ridges, amongst silver-tongued skylarks and blue butterflies. Then, head full of possibilities and effervescent light, I would race home to distil them onto paper. I painted for long hours; often, especially before dawn, to the accompaniment of the crows that feud over the tall chimney above my studio.

Once, like many teenagers of a certain disposition, I was given to writing overwrought poetry. I must have been about nineteen when my late grandfather said to me, from a hospital bed, 'keep writing your poetry, son'. Even I could tell that my painting was more viable than my verse so I kept doing that instead, and I have always felt a faint guilt at having ignored his advice. Today though, I hope he would approve of the poetry, both literary and visual, that we have conjured in these pages.

From bible-black crow to ozone-white gulls, these birds and words have carried me on a dazzling flight into language and letters, colour and light. I wouldn't have missed it for the world.

NG

ACKNOWLEDGEMENTS

Increasingly, as this book has taken shape, I've felt like a minor partner, watching on benevolently as the real geniuses set to work. Collaborating with Neil Gower has been an extraordinary honour — out of the back and forth of words and images a great and enduring friendship has grown. It will be a wrench to return to the black-and-white of my novels.

Karolina Sutton, my agent, deserves much of the credit for turning a few half-formed ideas into a carefully-structured book. She's one in a million.

The team at Corsair and Little, Brown has been brilliantly efficient, hugely supportive. I want particularly to thank my editor, James Gurbutt, a fellow-birder and author whose enthusiasm for this project has been so important to Neil and me. Sarah Castleton and Olivia Hutchings have been alongside us every step of the way, their efficiency, good humour and exquisite taste make me want to put their names on the cover. When James, Neil and I first sat down to discuss this book, I told them that I needed, above all, for it to be beautiful. Nico Taylor's patience and vision have played a huge role in making this the ravishing object you hold in your hands. The tub-thumping of our publicist, Grace Vincent, has ensured that the book not only exists, but might actually be read.

I must thank my parents for the long and, I imagine, terribly boring hours they spent beside me in bird hides and on bleak estuaries. My aunts Jo and Gay for nurturing a love of birds and nature. Finally, as ever, my love and gratitude to Ary, Al and Ray, who are everything.

NOTES

INTRODUCTION

1 Jonathan Franzen, 'My Bird Problem', *The New Yorker*.
2 Bach's gull pursues flying for the thrill of it and is fond of spouting gnomic sixties stuff like 'We're free to go where we wish and to be what we are'; and 'You have the freedom to be yourself, your true self, here and now, and nothing can stand in your way. It is the Law of the Great Gull, the Law that Is.'
3 J.A. Baker, *The Peregrine*.
4 In his 2005 *New Yorker* article, Jonathan Franzen describes a discussion with a friend who gives the kind of response I envisaged the (largely imaginary) girls of my early teens giving to the news that I was a bird nerd:

> I told her I'd been looking at birds. 'No, no, no, no, no, no,' she said. 'You are not going to be a bird-watcher.'
> 'Why not?'
> 'Because bird-watchers − *ucch*. They're all so − *ucch*.'
> 'But if I'm doing it,' I said, 'and if I'm not that way −'
> 'But that's the thing!' she said. 'You're going to become that way. And then I won't want to see you anymore.'

5 That specular felo-de-se has haunted me. So too, it would seem, Joanna Newsom in 'Only Skin':

> Last week our picture window produced a half-word
> Heavy and hollow, hit by a brown bird.

6 I have, for instance, omitted the cuckoo − I found nothing beyond Hopkins's 'Repeat that, repeat' in my notebooks, and while I wrote and re-wrote the chapter, I just couldn't make it work.
7 Gillian Clarke, 'Curlew'.
8 Translation by Arthur Waley.

PEREGRINE

1 'The Needles,' writes Patrick Barkham in *Coastlines*, 'which attract peregrines, fog and scenic television shots.'
2 Its name is explained by Ali Smith in *How to Be Both*: 'The peregrine falcon, her mother'd said, Pellegrino means a pilgrim, and at some point it also morphed into what we know as the name of the bird.'
3 Which Macfarlane enumerates beautifully in *Landmarks*, after having given us his best Baker impression: 'Intersection, shrapnel of down, grey drop to crop, ail and clatter, four chops and the black star away with quick wing flicks.'
4 Macfarlane's *Landmarks* goes some way in demystifying the man: he worked for the AA, lived with his wife Doreen (a fellow AA employee), suffered from ankylosing spondylitis,

which results in the fusing together of bones and is incurable and horribly painful. He was also near-blind (perhaps as a result of his illness). *The Peregrine*, rather than the record of one winter (which is how it's presented), is actually the compression of ten years of diaries into a single year.

5   Walter Benjamin said in an essay on Proust that 'all great works of literature establish a genre or dissolve one.' *The Peregrine* is neither memoir, nor nature writing, nor narrative non-fiction, nor novel.

6   In a discussion at Stanford University with Professor Robert Harrison (available on Stanford's YouTube channel), Werner Herzog spoke about *The Peregrine*, which is one of three books that students at his Rogue Film School are required to have read (the others are Virgil's *Georgics* and Ernest Hemingway's 'The Short Happy Life of Francis Macomber'). Herzog said that 'The intensity and the ecstasy of observation is something that you have to have as a filmmaker or somebody who loves literature. Whoever really loves literature, whoever really loves movies, should read that book.'

7   Sanderling. The name comes from the old English sand-yrðling, meaning sand-ploughman.

SWALLOW

1   Ted Hughes, 'A Swallow'.
2   From an essay published posthumously in *The Guardian* in May 2015.
3   Joanna Newsom, interview with *Vogue*, October 2015.
4   Ted Hughes, 'Work and Play'.
5   Kathleen Jamie, 'The Swallows' Nest'.
6   Tim Dee, *The Running Sky: A Bird-Watching Life*.
7   Thomas Carew, poetic arbiter elegantiae of the court of Charles I, went one further, figuring the swallow as a kind of phoenix, woken by the rays of the spring sun:
     But the warm sun thaws the benumbed earth,
     And makes it tender; gives a sacred birth
     To the dead swallow.
8   Leonora Speyer, 'Swallows'.
9   William Stafford, 'The Well Rising'.
10   Translation by Ashley Dukes.
11   Tim Dee, *The Running Sky: A Bird-Watching Life*.
12   In 'Swallows I'.

KINGFISHER

1   In her very fine introduction to *The Penguin Book of Bird Poetry*, Peggy Munsterberg identifies 'Upon Appleton House' as the first work to contain modern, 'realistic glimpses of birds', rather than the allegorical, anthropomorphic figures of Romance and Elizabethan poetry.

2   Eliot was a keen birder whose poem 'Cape Ann' is one of the loveliest evocations of the joy of birdwatching. According to his letters, the kingfisher in Burnt Norton was based on a bird he saw on the River Trent, near Kelham.

3   It was Milton, in 'On the Morning of Christ's Nativity', who linked the Greek idea of halcyon days – a period of calm around the winter solstice in which kingfishers were thought to nest upon the ocean – with Christmas. He writes of the peace on the night the 'Prince of Light' was born, 'While Birds of Calm sit brooding on the charmed wave.' Gerard Manley Hopkins deepens the bird's religious associations in the first line of one of his most famous poems, 'As Kingfishers Catch Fire'. The sonnet, written in 1877, uses the kingfisher's shimmering flight to illustrate Hopkins's belief, taken from Duns Scotus, that 'Christ plays in ten thousand places'.

4   Joanna Newsom does something similar in 'Kingfisher':

> Stand here and name
> the one you loved,
> beneath the drifting ashes,
> and, in naming, rise above time,
> as it, flashing, passes.

5 Chris McCabe, 'Kingfisher'.
6 In his *Notes on the Natural History of Norfolk*, Sir Thomas Browne refers to 'that handsome coloured bird' who nests in holes 'wherein is to be found great quantity of small fish bones.'

KESTREL

1 Robert Macfarlane notes in *Landmarks* that one dialect name for the kestrel is 'wind-fucker' and 'it is hard now not to see in the pose of the hovering kestrel a certain lustful quiver.' In *The Wild Places*, Macfarlane sees a 'kestrel riding the wind, its wings shivering with the strain, its tail feathers spread out like a hand of cards.' The kestrel – randy, gambling, loutish.
2 In flight, the kestrel looks like a football hooligan's rattle. *Kestrel*, from the French *crécelle* (ratchet) conjures the hovering shape of the bird, the diver's tuck it tightens itself into prior to a strike, the long tail splayed like a tongue tasting the wind.
3 Michael Longley, 'Kestrel'.
4 T.H. White, *The Goshawk*.
5 Wilkinson parses bating as: 'To beat the wings impatiently and flutter away from the fist or pouch.'
6 T.H. White's words from *The Goshawk*.
7 Don Paterson, in 'Goldberg and Piskey in Cornwall', conjures a kestrel 'keeping itself still (so the world is the biggest sentence, hung off the tiniest, prettiest comma).'
8 Thoreau is driven to similar raptures by the bird's flight in this passage from *Walden*:
   > it sported with proud reliance in the fields of air; mounting again and again with its strange chuckle, it repeated its free and beautiful fall, turning over and over like a kite, and then recovering from its lofty tumbling, as if it had never set its foot on terra firma. It appeared to have no companion in the universe, – sporting there alone, – and to need none but the morning and the ether with which it played. It was not lonely, but made all the earth lonely beneath it.
9 The ridges between plough-furrows.
10 I'm already horribly aware of the extent to which Hughes will be one of the dominant voices this book. I can only say that he's played such an important part in my own life, his poems a crutch and an inspiration, his words providing a direct path into nature, and to the vision of my young self reading him and loving him.
11 You can see the way that Hopkins's 'Windhover' echoes down through the poems of Hughes and Sidney Keyes – the bird and the plough (or 'plow' in Keyes) have been laced together in Hopkins and find themselves repeated in the later poets' work.

GULL

1 Reprinted in *On Wings of Song: Poems About Birds*.
2 Seagulls, of course, do not exist, as any pedantic ornithologist will tell you. They are gulls, *tout court*.
3 I recognised these birds when I read David Flusfeder's *A Film by Spencer Ludwig*. The hero spots an injured gull and 'forces his unwilling hands to pick up the bird, which flaps even harder now. He had not realized quite how wide a seagull's wingspan is ...The seagull's heart beats against his chest as Spencer scurries to the safety of the sidewalk.'
4 Both collected in *Up in the Old Hotel*.
5 Geraldine Monk writes of great black-backed gulls: 'When your heavy weight darkens a sky / lighter things scud for cover.'

6 Cook died in 2005. The two had been almost literally inseparable over the course of their forty-year relationship.
7 The portrayal of his father has been fiercely questioned by numerous critics and biographers. What is important is that this is what it felt like to Gosse.

STARLING

1 Ted Hughes, 'Starlings Have Come'.
2 Coleridge was obsessed by the sight of flocking starlings, writing at length of them in his diaries, seizing upon the image of the birds as a powerful manifestation of the sublime – both in their mind-swamping numbers and in the overwhelming beauty of their shifting, shimmering flight.
    Starlings in vast flights drove along like smoke, mist, or any thing misty without volition – now a circular area inclined in an Arc – now a Globe – now from complete Orb into an Elipse & Oblong – now a balloon with the car suspended, now a concaved Semicircle – & still it expands & condenses, some moments glimmering & shivering, dim & shadowy, now thickening, deepening, blackening!
3 James McAuley, 'Starlings'.
4 Jesper Svenbro, 'The Starlings'.
5 From the Old English *staer*, becoming *stare* until the 1500s, when it was replaced by starling (which was previously used to describe the juvenile bird). Yeats employs the archaic form in his poem 'The Stare's Nest By My Window', while John Clare calls them starnels.
6 'That was beautiful.'

WREN

1 'It is many years since my sight enabled me to observe birds by eye, except when very close to me, but my recollection is that the tree-creeper opens the beak very widely to sing,' he writes early on in the book.
2 The Grey family seat.
3 It is pheasant season as I'm writing this, and I can hear guns in the distance. They call to mind Alexander Pope's lines in *Windsor Forest*, published in 1713.
    See! from the brake the whirring pheasant springs,
    And mounts exulting on triumphant wings:
    Short is his joy; he feels the fiery wound,
    Flutters in blood, and, panting, beats the ground.
    Ah! what avail his glossy, varying dyes,
    His purple crest, and scarlet-circled eyes,
    The vivid green his shining plumes unfold,
    His painted wings, and breast that flames with gold?
4 Whom he and Dorothy revered. He referred to the poet rather winningly as 'Big Daddy'.
5 Grey's life was about to be heaped with more tragedy: within a year of the publication of *The Charm of Birds*, his second wife, Pamela Tennant, would be dead and his brother Charles mauled to death by a buffalo while big game hunting in Africa. It left Edward the last of the four boys alive – George Grey was eaten by a lion in 1911, while Harry Alexander Grey died after a botched operation in 1914.
6 'Cock wrens . . . mak[e] half a dozen exquisite play nests before the big performance that is meant to lure their mate. In and out go the meticulously woven moss and feathers, round the little entrance John Clare likened to "a crock-hole in a barrel." But it is all so much bachelor stuff, done for practice, amusement and showing off.' Richard Mabey, *Nature Cure*.
7 James Grahame, 'Birds of Scotland'.
8 Wordsworth, 'The Contrast'.
9 Tim Dee, *The Running Sky: A Bird-Watching Life*.

10 Ted Hughes, 'Wren'.
11 In *The Big Issue*, June 2012.
12 Ted Hughes, 'Wren'.

SKYLARK

1 Hardy may have read this note, imagining in his poem, 'Shelley's Skylark', that the bird, long dead, now 'throbs in a myrtle's green'.
2 This image picks up on the lark in Goethe's *Faust*: 'When far above us pours its thrilling song / The skylark, lost in azure light.'
3 In 'Resolution and Independence', where the skylark makes a fleeting cameo, Wordsworth writes that 'We poets in our youth begin in gladness; / But thereof come in the end despondency and madness.'
4 Just as Hardy drew 'dewfell hawk' for his nightjar from Clare, his dust-speck skylark in 'Shelley's Skylark' nods to Clare as well as Shelley: 'A pinch of unseen, unguarded dust / The dust of the lark that Shelley heard.'
5 In 'To the Snipe' he writes of a primal need for solitude and secrecy:
    Places untrodden lye
    Where man nor boy nor stock hath ventured near
    − Nought gazed on but the sky

    And fowl that dread
    The very breath of man,
    Hiding in spots that never knew his tread −
    A wild and timid clan
6 When Clare tried to sign up as a militia man in the Napoleonic Wars, he was told he was too short, finally enlisting as a 'bum-tool', the lowest-ranked of the motley Northampton soldiery. Rosenberg enlisted in the 12th Bantam Battalion of the Suffolk Regiment, reserved for men under the height of five feet three inches.

NIGHTJAR

1 In *British Birds — their Folklore, Names and Literature,* Francesca Greenoak writes: 'Almost every night-bird superstition there is seems, in some time or place, to have been attached to the Nightjar. Like the Tawny Owl, it is known as the Corpse Bird or Lich (corpse) Fowl. It is also given the title Gabble Ratchet, a name for the Gabriel Hounds of the Wild Hunt. In Nidderdale in Yorkshire, there is a tradition that the souls of dead unbaptized children go into Nightjars.' Thoreau, on the other hand, dismissed the idea that nighthawks (the nightjar's American cousin) boded ill: 'Go into the woods in a warm night at this season,' he wrote in his journal in June 1851, 'and it [the churring of the bird] is the prevailing sound. I hear now five or six at once. It is no more of ill omen therefore here than the night and the moonlight are.' He also calls it an 'imp of darkness', though.
2 About whom Claudia Renton wrote in *Those Wild Wyndhams: Three Sisters at the Heart of Power.*
3 In *Strangers*, Emma Tennant, Eddy and Pamela's grand-daughter, writes: 'Eddy knows, without of course it ever being mentioned, that his wife will marry Grey and live at Fallodon should anything happen to him. He and the other Edward are already seen as Pamela's two husbands: sometimes he thinks it would not matter at all if he simply slipped away.' Sure enough, Eddy Tennant died in 1920, aged sixty-one, and Grey and Pamela married in 1922.
4 Newbolt was 'more Victorian than the queen', according to Robert Fulford.
5 Newbolt's entry in *Who's Who* listed his favourite recreation as 'bird-nesting'.
6 Angela Lambert in *Unquiet Souls* said: 'Pamela found the love of her life in another Edward, later Lord Grey of Fallodon, and the three of them lived in a discreet ménage à trois which

lasted until Lord Glenconner's [Eddy Tennant's] death.'

7   Where Newbolt would eventually be buried.

8   Described by Jonathan Franzen in *The New Yorker* as looking like a 'partly-rolled gray hiking sock'.

9   Like Thoreau, who in *Walden* says that the nighthawk is 'so one with the earth, so Sphinx-like, a relic of the reign of Saturn which Jupiter did not destroy, a riddle that might well cause a man to go dash his head against a stone.'

10   Tim Dee goes for beer rather than wine: 'The sun falls and the nightjar's churring rises, like the moon, except this night there wasn't a moon, only a black vibration from deep inside a bird, like a stream of stout pouring from a tap, switched on to run at full pelt instantaneously, switched off equally abruptly. It goes like an engine, yet it is one of the most pre-industrial sounds you can imagine. Its motor is the underworld of the earth.'

11   The final missing 'end' weaves us back into the first line of the album's first song, 'Anecdotes':

> Sending the first scouts over,
> back from the place beyond the dawn.

SWIFT

1   Robert MacFarlane, *The Old Ways*.

2   Robert MacFarlane, *The Old Ways*.

3   In Jonathan Franzen's *Freedom*, Walter Berglund also wants to be a bird. I was reviewing the book for the BBC, and remember copying this passage into one of my notebooks on the plane up to Glasgow (where we recorded the show):

> He watched a catbird hopping around in an azalea that was readying itself to bloom; he envied the bird for knowing nothing of what he knew; he would have swapped souls with it in a heartbeat. And then to take wing, to know the air's buoyancy even for an hour: the trade was a no-brainer, and the catbird, with its lively indifference to him, its sureness of physical selfhood, seemed well aware of how preferable it was to be the bird.

4   In 'Swifts' Anne Stevenson writes about the joy that comes with the arrival of the birds: 'But one day the swifts are back. Face to the sun like a child / You shout, "The swifts are back!"'

5   William Fiennes, *The Snow Geese*.

6   Charles Foster, *Being a Beast*.

PEACOCK

1   It's like one of Yeats's 'Ancestral Houses', with 'gardens where the peacock strays / With delicate feet upon old terraces . . . '

2   Flannery O'Connor, 'Making the Introductions'.

3   Hardy, whom I admired so much, and who helped me make one of the most important decisions of my life, died as I was writing this book.

4   Flannery O'Connor used to dream of being eaten as a peacock. In 'Making the Introductions' she wrote: 'Lately I have had a recurrent dream: I am five years old and a peacock. A photographer has been sent from New York and a long table is laid in celebration. The meal is to be an exceptional one: myself. I scream, "Help! Help !" and awaken. Then from the pond and the barn and the trees around the house, I hear that chorus of jubilation begin.'

GOLDFINCH

1   The collective name for the goldfinch is indeed charm, but this is for their song, rather than any providential qualities, as Cecilia Woloch reminds us in 'For the Birds: A Charm of Goldfinches': 'a flock / of such birds called a *charm*, / from the Latin *Carmen*, meaning *song.*'
2   Hudson is one of those authors whose work is a staple of the market town's second-hand book store. The copies I've picked up from Rye, Banbury and Oxford were all lovingly inscribed, well-thumbed, covered in dust and melancholy.
3   There are many parallels between Hudson and Richard Jefferies. Both were wanderers upon, and lovers of the South Downs; both wrote science-fiction with a strong environmental bent; both suffered with their chests and moved to Worthing for the air (also the reason that we lived there – I was a wheezy child); both are buried at Broadwater Cemetery in the town, although Hudson's grave lies largely untended while Jefferies' was smart and flower-strewn when I last visited a few months ago.
4   Collected here is a euphemism for 'shot'. One of the best passages in Wilson's book about Hudson describes the way that binoculars brought about an epiphany for the naturalist. He was able to see birds close-up without harming them – 'of all man's inventions, this is to me the most like a divine gift,' he wrote. Hudson's antipathy to pheasant and wild goose shooting became a central facet of his character; his dislike of the upper classes (Grey excepted) stemmed as much from his distaste for their ritual slaughter of birds as from his natural, radical democratic spirit.
5   The goldfinch's name in German, Der Stieglitz, means 'rising one'.
6   Osip Mandelstam called himself 'Goldfinch' and wrote four poems about the bird during his exile in Voronezh between 1935–37. The poems were preserved by his wife and Anna Akhmatova (who memorised them, since publication was prohibited). The best of them is called 'The Cage'. In *On Tyranny*, an essay on Mandelstam, Joseph Brodsky said: 'His became a poetry of high velocity and exposed nerves, with numerous leaps over the self-evident with somewhat abbreviated syntax, and yet in this way it became more a song than ever before, not a bardlike but a birdlike song, with its sharp, unpredictable turns and pitches, something like a goldfinch tremolo.'

>   When the goldfinch like rising dough
>   suddenly moves, as a heart throbs,
>   anger peppers its clever cloak
>   and its nightcap blackens with rage.
>
>   The cage is a hundred bars of lies
>   the perch and little plank are slanderous.
>   Everything in the world is inside out,
>   and there is the Salamanca forest
>   for disobedient, clever birds.
>   (from *The Voronezh Notebooks*. Translated by Richard and Elizabeth McKane.)

7   He wouldn't be that man for long, though. Giovanni de' Medici died of malaria with his mother and brother in 1562, aged just nineteen.
8   Hitchcock's term: an object around which the plot revolves.
9   This too is a caged bird. Theo notices that the goldfinch is 'chained to a perch by its twig of an ankle'.

ROBIN

1   David Lack was Director of the Edward Grey Institute at Oxford University.
2   'Robin, I watch you. You are a perfect robin,' Norman MacCaig writes in 'Real-Life Christmas Carol', 'except, shouldn't you be perched on a spade handle?'
3   In the way of these things, I've found out since that Reverend Green was an incorrigible shagger, his MG Midget parked daily in front of the cottage of any one of a dozen local ladies

while their husbands were out at work or in the fields. He was asked to leave his position after a particularly public and riotous affair with the Sunday School teacher.

4   A different bird – the American robin, of course – but one whose iconography shares much with its European namesake.

5   Who wrote as Fiona Macleod, a female pseudonym that grew out of his affair with one of his wife's friends, Edith Wingate Rinder. Sharp's creation of Macleod was at first an attempt to forge a closer spiritual connection to his lover. Fiona Macleod's work proved more popular than that of William Sharp, and Sharp found himself trapped as Macleod for the rest of his writing life.

6   Strange to think that such an English novel first appeared on the other side of the Atlantic. It wasn't published in Britain until 1911.

GREY HERON

1   John Leyden, 'Albania'.
2   'so still that I believe / he is a bit of drift hung dead above the water.' Wendell Berry, 'The Heron'.
3   Mary Oliver, 'Heron Rising From the Dark, Summer Pond'.
4   Dylan Thomas, 'Poem in October'.
5   He also points out that Peter Matthiessen's *The Birds of Heaven: Travels with Cranes*, uses as its epigraph a John Clare poem that is actually about a heron.
6   It's worth recalling Paul Farley's brilliant description of the 'begrudging avian take-off'.
7   Vernon Watkins, 'The Heron'.
8   Paul Farley, 'The Heron'.
9   J.A. Baker, 'The Peregrine'.
10 W.B. Yeats, 'Motionless Under the Moon-Beam'.

CROW

1   'If I had to go for any length of time with that feeling I'd surely kill myself,' Day says. Wallace, a brave, damaged, beautiful man, lived under the wing for most of his life, until he hanged himself in his garage on 12 September 2008. I was with my grandparents in Princeton and, for want of any better venue for my mourning, walked to the tennis courts, then to the book store on Nassau Street, where I bought a copy of *Brief Interviews With Hideous Men*, even though I'd already read it.

2   In *All the Birds Singing,* Evie Wyld populates the bleak island home of her heroine, Jake, with crows, undercutting the nod to Edward Thomas in the book's title on the first page: 'Crows, their beaks shining, strutting and rasping, and when I waved my stick they flew to the trees and watched, flaring out their wings, singing, if you could call it that.' Jake shouts 'What are you laughing at?' and lobs a rock at them.

3   Crows are the sinister familiars of Selina Place – the Morrigan – the villain of Alan Garner's *The Weirdstone of Brisingamen*. It was my favourite book as a child, and now my children love it fiercely. There are ravens and carrion crows throughout the novel, all in the service of the evil Morthbrood. It's a crow that calls up the svart alfar, a swarm of dark elves, and crows stalk the children as they seek to return the stone to Cadellin Silverbrow. At the end of the novel, after an epic battle, the Morrigan, defeated, turns herself into a crow:

> Selina Place, fury in every line of her, shrieked, and ran. And as she ran a change came over her. She seemed to bend low over the ground, and she grew smaller; her robes billowed out at her side; her thin legs were thinner, her squat body heavier; and then there was no Selina Place, only a carrion crow rising into a sky of jet.

4   Translated by Sasha Dugdale.
5   In *Poets on Poets*, edited by Nick Rennisopn and Michael Schmidt.

6   I'd argue with 'anthropomorphic'; it seems to me that Hughes is trying to leap the species barrier entirely in his poems, to give crow a voice that is truly his. These are anti-human poems.

7   Ian Bamforth, 'Pickled Essence of Englishman'.

8   The origin of the poems was, like this book, a collaboration between an artist and an author. In 'Crow on the Beach', Hughes wrote that *Crow* grew out of an invitation by Leonard Baskin to make a book with him.

> He wanted an occasion to add more crows to all the crows that flock through his sculpture, drawings, and engravings in their various transformations. As the protagonist of a book, a crow would become symbolic in any author's hands. And a symbolic crow lives a legendary life. That is how *Crow* took off.

CURLEW

1   Clare muses at one point that this beautiful bird might have been named the golden curlew, and had its sad fate altered through the nomenclatural aura.

2   Ezra Pound renders 'Huilpan' as 'Sea-fowl' in his translation but most others agree it's a curlew. The curlew is still called a 'whaup' in the North of England, and Margaret Goldsmith, in her definitive *The Seafarer and the Birds*, argues convincingly that the Huilpan is a curlew.

3   Richard Mabey, *A Brush With Nature*.

4   Francesca Greenoak, in *British Birds – their Folklore, Names and Literature*, notes that in South Shropshire and Worcestershire, six curlews are said to be searching for their lost brother. When they find him, the world will end.

5   For ornithological exactitude, the poem ought probably to have been titled 'The Bush Stone Curlew Cried'.

6   Quoted in Branda Carr Vellino, '"Their embassies were everywhere": Amnesty International and Seamus Heaney's Ambassadors of Conscience'.

7   This is despite the fact that the bird was removed from the official register of quarry species as part of the 1981 Wildlife and Countryside Act, with one MP stating the case for exclusion thus: 'The curlew has such a lovely call.' It is habitat destruction that threatens them, just as it wiped out two of their cousins.

8   William Atkins, *The Moor*.

WAXWING

1   In his novel *Waxwings*, Jonathan Raban notes that 'The birds were better than their pictures – trim dandies, the sheen of their plumage bright beyond reason in the gloomy overcast.'

2   It's the only one of Nabokov's books which features more avian life than lepidopteran. There are thirteen birds and only three butterflies. Nabokov also seemed to take on the spirit of a bird in writing the novel:

> All I know is that at a very early stage of the novel's development, I get this urge to gather bits of straw and fluff and eat pebbles. Nobody will ever discover how closely a bird visualizes, or if it visualizes at all, the future nest and the eggs in it.
> (Quoted in Brian Boyd, *Vladimir Nabokov: The American Years*.)

3   Brian Boyd notes that the author took the figure of the suicidal waxwing from life. In October 1957, three years before he began work on *Pale Fire*, Nabokov would be sitting in his study and:

> from time to time feel a thud shake the whole house. Just in front of the ... large picture window stood some rosebushes. At this time of year cedar waxwings often became quite drunk on the swelling rose hips, and flew into the window. Normally they would simply stun themselves, although occasionally they might break their necks.

4   Jonathan Raban also describes the birds feasting on fermented fruit until they can't see straight. 'Some of them get so drunk on the berries that they fall out of the trees, too heavy to fly. You see them lying on their backs, sozzled out of their tiny minds with their feet waving in the air.'

5   In many of their southerly distributions, Britain included, waxwings are not regular visitors, but appear in irruptions, largely driven by the failure of their native Scandinavian and north Russian fruit crops. In the 'great invasion' of the winter of 1946/47, 12,500 birds were seen in the UK. By the winter of 1948/49, the number had fallen to 200.

6   Unlucky-bird or death-bird.

7   Reminding us of the lines from Nabokov: 'I / Lived on, flew on, in the reflected sky.'

8   In *Modern Poetry in Translation*, Sasha Dugdale says that Khlebnikov writes 'moving poems about the natural world with the depth of vision of the poet John Clare.'

9   Dugdale translates *zaum* as: 'a word coined by the Russian Futurists meaning literally "beyond the brain"; often translated as "transrational". In poetic practice it sometimes refers to work we might describe as "nonsense verse".'

10 Quoted by Dugdale in *Modern Poetry Today*.

11 T.S. Eliot, *The Sacred Wood*.

12 Translated by Tatiana Tulchinsky, Andrew Wachtel and Gwenan Wilbur.

13 Elsewhere, these birds are translated as 'time-finches', 'timelings' and 'mockingbird minutes'.

14 Commemorated in 'Gul-Mullah's Trumpet'.

COLLARED DOVE

1   As I'm typing this, my wife comes in to tell me that Prince has died. It's unexpected and dismantling. I put on 'When Doves Cry' and we shiver at those opening yowls of his guitar.

2   Michael Longley, 'War & Peace'.

3   Their official name in German is *Die Türketaube*, the Turkish dove, or, more colloquially, *Die Fernsehtaube*, the television dove, for their habit of perching on aerials.

4   In 'Mural', Mahmoud Darwish writes: 'Heroes have their eagles, / mine is a ring-necked dove.'

5   'Little Gidding' ends with an image that seeks to resolve the paradox that runs throughout the *Four Quartets*. The severity of the dove fuses with the softness of the rose and, quoting Julian of Norwich, Eliot kneads the poem's end into its beginning, with the urgent bird leading us into the rose garden.

>   And all shall be well and
>   All manner of thing shall be well
>   When the tongues of flame are in-folded
>   Into the crowned knot of fire
>   And the fire and the rose are one.

6   Although, after a first sighting in Miami in 1982, the Eurasian collared dove is now spreading across the USA with the same marauding energy it brought to its colonisation of Europe.

7   An association that comes up more clearly in the wretched lines of 'Dove in Spring', written when Stevens was close to the age of my father. Here, the dove 'Makes this small howling, like a thought / That howls in the mind or like a man / Who keeps seeking out his identity.' The dove is sexual desire grown bitter, turned inward with age, and its howling, though small, keeps the poet from sleep. 'Enforced celibacy,' wrote my father, his son reading through squeamish fingers, 'not challenging at his age, soon led to loss of libido. The old man interpreted the loss, when the issue opened its ugly eye, as a benefit of his condition.'

8   I wonder now whether this third-person mode of writing about himself was a way of my dad putting distance between him and his own rebellious body.

9   '. . . why, if I pause to listen, should the languageless note of a dove / So dark with disquietude seem? And what is it sorrowing of?' Walter de la Mare, 'The Dove'.

10 This reminded me of Simon Barnes, who described the doves as 'neat, pretty birds that look ever so slightly like angels when they take off'.

SNOW GOOSE

1   Michael Longley, 'Snow Geese'.
2   He has since written in graceful detail about his Crohn's disease, the horrors of his treatment and the shadow it cast across his young life.
3   I'm reminded of the birds that arrive on the harsh heathland of Flintcombe-Ashe in *Tess of the D'Urbevilles*, omens of the ills to come for Tess, but perhaps also emblems of resilience and resistance, to let her know how much is survivable in this parlous and contingent world:
> After this season of congealed dampness came a spell of dry frost, when strange birds from behind the North Pole began to arrive silently on the upland of Flintcombe-Ashe, gaunt spectral creatures with tragical eyes – eyes which had witnessed scenes of cataclysmal horror in inaccessible polar regions of a magnitude such as no human being had ever conceived, in curdling temperatures that no man could endure; which had beheld the crash of icebergs and the slide of snowhills by the shooting light of the Aurora; been half blinded by the whirl of colossal storms and terraqueous distortions; and retained the expression of feature that such scenes had engendered. These nameless birds came quite near Tess and Marian, but of all they had seen which humanity would never see, they brought no account.

BARN OWL

1   It looked just like Eric Ravilous's woodcut of Gilbert White's barn owl in my Little Toller Press edition of *The Natural History of Selborne*.
2   In *The Natural History of Selborne*, White, who must have felt a familial connection to the owls that shared his name, wrote:
> We have had ever since I can remember, a pair of white owls that constantly breed under the eaves of this church ... About an hour before sunset (for then the mice begin to run) they sally forth in quest of prey, and hunt all round the hedges of meadows and small enclosures for them, which seem to be their only food. In this irregular country we can stand on an eminence and see them beat the fields over like a setting dog, and often drop down in the grass or corn ... The white owl does indeed snore and hiss in a tremendous manner; and these menaces well answer the intention of intimidating: for I have known a whole village up in arms on such an occasion, imagining the church-yard to be full of goblins and spectres.

3   Pliny described the barn owl as 'the very monster of the night' and argued that 'when it appears, it foretells nothing but evil'. Barn owls were burnt as witches in the Middle Ages; farmers used to nail dead owls to barn doors to ward off evil spirits.
4   Richard Mabey, *A Brush With Nature*.
5   Barn owls suffered terribly from the use of pesticides in the 1950s and 1960s, as well as from loss of hunting territory.
6   Translated by Roy Campbell.
7   R.S. Thomas, 'Barn Owl'.
8   Woolf loved barn owls. Eleanor Partiger in Woolf's last novel, *The Years*, watches the bird rather than listening to sordid family gossip. The owl reappears throughout the novel as Eleanor ages, drawing her away from the social world and towards the natural. 'She wanted to see the owl before it got too dark. She was becoming more and more interested in birds. It was a sign of old age, she supposed, as she went into her bedroom. An old maid who washes and watches birds.' In Woolf's diaries, she recounts an August evening where she and Leonard sat on the terrace at Monk's House. 'We were watching the downs draw back into fine darkness after they had burnt like solid emerald all day. Now that was being softly finely veiled. And the white owl was crossing to fetch mice from the marsh.'
9   Not a barn owl, but I loved *The Outrun* so much, I thought you'd allow me this.
10 John Hollander, 'Owl'.

NIGHTINGALE

1   Nightingales arrive in April and are largely gone by the end of July.
2   In *Resurgence*.
3   Anna Akhmatova, 'As a Silver, Delicate Strand', translated by A.S. Kline.
4   Tomas Tranströmer, 'The Nightingale in Badelunda', translated by Robin Fulton.
5   In *Whistling in the Dark*, his beautiful book about nightingales, Richard Mabey listens to a
     nightingale who appears to summon the stars down from the sky.
     > He is louder and more extravagant now, and seems to be rehearsing the whole
     > nightingale repertoire. He sings a stylish four-note phrase, then repeats it in a minor
     > key. He slides into a bubbling tremolo on a single note and holds it for more than ten
     > seconds. How does he breathe? I cannot believe he is not consciously improvising. I want
     > to clap – and with barely credible timing, a shooting star arcs over the bush in which he
     > is singing.
6   'I can sit at my window here & hear the nightingale singing in the orchard & I attempted to
     take down her notes but they are so varied that every time she starts again after the pauses
     seems to be somthing different to what she utterd before & many of her notes are sounds
     that cannot be written the alphabet having no letters than can syllable the sounds.'
     > Quoted in Hugh Haughton, *John Clare in Context*.
7   A neume from Gregorian chant.
8   Olivier Messaein, *On Birds*, my translation.
9   I'm still very fond of the poem, though. It was a relief, arriving at Oxford and feeling
     that everyone had read so much more than me, to write my first essay on nightingales in
     Romantic verse, calling up birds that I knew intimately from their place on the pages of my
     Penguin Book of Bird Poetry.
10   Vladimir Nabokov associated his poetry with the nightingale, although here the bird is
     straying towards Romantic pastiche, as the author looks back on his earliest poems, whose
     > natural environment was characterized by nightingales in tears, lilacs in bloom and the
     > alleys of whispering trees that graced the parks of the landed gentry. Those nightingales
     > trilled, and in a pine grove the setting sun banded the trunks at different levels with fiery
     > red. A tambourine, still throbbing, seemed to lie on the darkening moss.
11   Ted Hughes, *Tales from Ovid*.
12   T.S. Eliot, 'The Waste Land'.
13   See, amongst others, Lyly's 'Ode to a Nightingale': 'Jug, jug, jug, jug, tereu, she cries, / And
     still her woes at midnight rise.'
14   Virginia Woolf, *The Waves*.
15   Verlaine, 'The Nightingale', translated by A.S. Kline.
16   Wallace Stevens, 'Autumn Refrain'.
17   Wallace Stevens, 'Autumn Refrain'.
18   Rossetti asked in 'Twilight Calm' why we assume that the bird's call is mournful.
     > We call it love and pain
     > The passion of her strain;
     > And yet we little understand or know;
     > Why should it not be rather joy that so
     > Throbs in each throbbing vein?